THE FIRST FIVE YEARS OF THE PRIESTHOOD

The First Five Years of the Priesthood

A Study of Newly Ordained Catholic Priests

Dean R. Hoge

THE LITURGICAL PRESS
Collegeville, Minnesota

www.litpress.org

Cover design by David Manahan, O.S.B. Photo by The Crosiers, Gene Plaisted, O.S.C.

1	2	3	4	5	6	7	8

Library of Congress Cataloging-in-Publication Data

Hoge, Dean R., 1937–
    The first five years of the priesthood : a study of newly ordained Catholic priests / Dean R. Hoge.
        p. cm.
    Includes bibliographical references and index.
    ISBN 0-8146-2804-4
    1. Catholic Church—United States—Clergy—Psychology. 2. Catholic ex-priests—United States—Psychology. 3. Priests—Psychology. I. Title.

BX1912 .H589 2002
262'.14273—dc21

2002067635

Contents

Foreword

Pulpit & Pew: An Introduction to the Project

This volume, *The First Five Years of the Priesthood,* is an important contribution to a larger research project, *Pulpit & Pew,* focused on pastoral leadership in Christian churches across the United States. *Pulpit & Pew: Research on Pastoral Leadership* is a project of Duke University Divinity School with funding from the Lilly Endowment, Inc.

We believe that pastoral leadership will be strengthened through better understanding of changes affecting ministry in recent years and by identifying policies and practices that support creative leadership and vital congregations in response to these changes. Thus *Pulpit & Pew* is pleased to collaborate with the National Federation of Priests' Councils in supporting research such as *The First Five Years of the Priesthood* to stimulate a conversation about pastoral leadership and the changes impacting it.

Three sets of questions are central to the purpose of *Pulpit & Pew:*

- What is the state of pastoral leadership at the new century's beginning, and what do current trends portend for the next generation?

- What is "good ministry"? Can we describe it? How does it come into being? Do its characteristics vary by denominational tradition? By congregational context?

- What can be done to help "good ministry" to come into being more frequently, and how can it be nurtured and supported more directly?

The research reported in this volume addresses these questions in important ways. Its findings and the various reflections on them should be of great help to the Catholic Church, but I am certain that leaders of Protestant denominations can also benefit from them. Likewise, I hope that other *Pulpit & Pew* research on Protestant clergy will be of interest and help to Catholic Church leaders. Although there are aspects of pastoral leadership unique to denominational traditions, many issues cut across these traditions. Thus I commend this book to you and express deep appreciation to its author, Professor Dean R. Hoge, and his staff for their careful, thoughtful, and stimulating research and interpretation of the findings.

Dr. Jackson W. Carroll

Director, *Pulpit & Pew*
Ruth W. & A. Morris Williams Professor Emeritus
Duke University Divinity School
www.pastoralleadership.duke.edu

Preface

One of the great wisdom figures of the Church in the United States was Monsignor Jack Egan, the venerable Chicago priest of social justice fame. As he lay dying in the cathedral rectory, he prayed for the ten men being ordained in the cathedral church next door. "God bless these new priests." He had often expressed concern for the newly ordained, recognizing that theirs was not to be an easy road. He was not alone in his concern.

The communities priests serve are complex. They are increasingly multicultural and multiethnic because of changing immigration patterns set off by the globalization process and the availability of accessible travel. The premodern, modern, and postmodern worlds exist side by side, each demanding attention. A new scientism challenges religion as the primary way of ordering reality. The Generation Xers and the millennialists are bringing new dynamics into American social systems.

The priest's role is to "make sense of the mess." He is to bring the light of the Gospel to the concrete situations of the current world. He is to discern and reflect the Spirit's movement in surfacing the kingdom in the reality of the everyday. He is to proclaim life in the face of death and despair, and to celebrate with thanksgiving the hope of resurrection that breaks through the shadow of life's underside.

No easy task! The sheer immensity of the priest's ministry is overwhelming. Many priests find themselves overburdened and overcome. Priests put in long hours. They mediate the conflicts caused by differing visions of the world and differing expectations placed on them. They live constantly off balance in a world of diverse cultures and languages. The sheer numbers of people with whom they minister is astonishing. They are bombarded with the seductions of a sexually liberated society as they attempt to live out their celibate lives.

Yet, in service of the ministry and the mission of Jesus, the priest is called to a life in which his relationships are healthy and fulfilling. He is, by vocation, to open himself to an intimacy that meets the deep needs of his heart. He is to practice a holiness that signs forth the love of God and a celibate life that witnesses to unconditional Love and singular commitment. He is to be a leader of God's Holy People.

In the practicalities of daily ministry, where ideals are tempered by life-situations, how does a newly ordained priest find himself? Is there a "fire in his belly" that drives him to engage the tradition and the world in a truly new and dynamic evangelization? Is he motivated to move beyond present day ecclesiastical structures? Does he have the courage to forsake ministerial practices that were developed for days past? Is he adventurous enough to search for an effective and passionate presbyterial ministry for the future? Can he be the priest, the presbyter, he is called to be?

Seven commentators give their reflections on this study, each bringing points for discussion and dialogue to the fore. The national conversation about priests, their place in the community, their ministry and their identity will be greatly helped by these thoughtful presentations. The context for such discussion is, of course, the mission of the Church in the present age.

The mission imposes a certain urgency for coming to some heightened understanding of the demands of a revitalized and impassioned presbyterial ministry for the Church in the United States. Sheer compassion in the face of such demands requires the ministerial community of priests and laity to envision together with the recently ordained a future Church in which presbyterial servant leadership flourishes. It will be together in the community of ministers, visioning and effecting a new evangelization and new ways of parish life, that the needs of the recently ordained will be fulfilled and transformed.

Hopefully this study will serve the purpose of fostering the dialogue. The National Federation of Priests' Councils seeks to provide a forum where ideas can be exchanged that lead to the revitalization of presbyterial life and the development of a renewed ministerial community. All who take up the study are invited to share in the exchange in both formal and informal settings.

Our gratitude goes out to Dean Hoge for his kindness, his wit, and his superb research skills. We acknowledge the generosity of those who wrote commentaries: Bishop Thomas Curry; Sr. Katarina Schuth, O.S.F.; Rev. Stephen Rossetti, Ph.D., D.Min.; Br. Loughlin Sofield, S.T.; Rev. James J. Gill, S.J., M.D.; Ms. Marti Jewell; and Rev. George Crespin. We are thankful to the Lilly Endowment and Duke University Divinity School's *Pulpit & Pew* project for their support and collaboration.

Rev. Robert J. Silva
President, The National Federation of Priests' Councils

Author's Preface

Early in 1999 the National Federation of Priests' Councils asked me if I and others at the Life Cycle Institute of Catholic University could begin a study of the problems of recently ordained Catholic priests. Reports were coming in from all sides that many newly ordained men were feeling demoralized and some were resigning. The accounts raised many questions. How widespread is the problem? What difficulties are the recently ordained priests facing? Is the problem due to changes in lay attitudes or to changes in the priests themselves? Is the situation different from what it was ten or twenty years ago?

The executive committee of the National Federation of Priests' Councils worked with me to design new research that would elicit information. We formed an advisory committee for the project; the members met twice during 1999–2000. In 1999 we formed a research group at the Life Cycle Institute that made a pilot survey of two groups—recently ordained priests active in service and those who had already resigned. Also, the research group interviewed five seminary rectors, gathered articles by observers, and commissioned preliminary essays by Katarina Schuth, Paul Rennick, Carol Stanton, and Bob Nohr.

On the basis of our early work, we decided to proceed with the overall project, and we subsequently received a grant from Dr. Jackson Carroll of Duke University Divinity School as part of a broad research program on clergy funded by the Lilly Endowment.

The pressure felt by recently ordained priests is a topic encumbered with already formed opinions. We researchers listened to viewpoints blaming the seminaries, the mentality of today's seminarians, and institutional policies. It became clear that the task of the research team was not to jump into the fray but merely to gather reliable new information that would make the debates more realistic and constructive. We decided to minimize interpretative work on our research findings and to engage credible voices in American Catholic life to write commentaries on the implications of the findings. This book is the result. It is a combination of research findings and commentaries. We hope and pray that it will be genuinely helpful.

The main part of the book has six chapters. The first chapter sets forth a brief summary of current data on Catholic seminaries, parishes, lay ministers, and other topics directly affecting the lives of newly ordained priests. It is needed in order that the reader can interpret the new research in view of the institutional climate of priestly life today. Chapter 2 presents the findings of our new surveys of active and resigned priests. Chapter 3 utilizes our survey data and interviews to help answer the question of why some newly ordained priests are happier than others, and Chapter 4 utilizes our data to try to understand why some priests have resigned. Chapter 5 pulls together revelatory information from our personal interviews on the priests' childhood experiences and the experiences since ordination. Finally, Chapter 6 summarizes the practical recommendations made by the priests we interviewed and then contributes a few reflections of our own on the entire project. The latter portion of the book contains commentaries by seven diverse observers of the Catholic priesthood and Catholic parish life.

Throughout the project we used research methods that promised to yield the most exact and reliable information possible and constrained our own interpretations of the findings as well as our own ideas about practical implications. Those are left to the commentators. Our entire effort was based on a value premise that was stated at the outset by the National Federation of Priests' Councils, namely, that a high level of priestly morale is to be desired and a large number of resignations is not to be desired. This premise underlay all our work. Any reader not sharing this premise is urged to read on and not put the book down, because our two years of research produced numerous rich findings of interest to everybody committed to the Catholic Church, regardless of ecclesiology.

I would like to thank the advisory committee—Melvin Blanchette, Michael Cronin, Robert Flagg, Ted Keating, Daniel Kidd, Cletus Kiley, Christa Klein, Lynn Levo, Stephen Rossetti, James Walsh, Donald Wolf, and Lea Woll—for their help and advice. I would also like to thank the staff of the National Federation of Priests' Councils for their good work, especially Bernard Stratman and Alan Szafraniec. The president of the National Federation of Priests' Councils, Robert Silva, gave encouragement and good counsel throughout.

At the Life Cycle Institute the principal project manager was Jacqueline Wenger, who had assistance from Patrick Lynch, Melissa Aujero, Meagan Schiavone, and Ding Kounian. I would like to thank Andrea Herdelin, Carol Stanton, Robert Burke, Thomas Butler, Ann McCleary, Edward Metz, James

Ivers, Rick Krivanka, and Roger Ridgeway for interviewing. Betty Seaver edited the manuscript and made many improvements.

Finally, we gratefully acknowledge Dr. Jackson Carroll of the Duke Divinity School and the Lilly Endowment for their financial support. Funding during the pretest phase was generously provided by Guest House, Inc., the Conference of Major Superiors of Men, the Society of St. Sulpice, and the Center for Continuing Formation at St. Mary's Seminary and University, Baltimore.

Dean Hoge
Autumn 2001

Chapter 1

The Setting of the Priesthood Today

This research was begun in response to numerous reports that newly ordained priests are feeling pressured today and are resigning at unaccept-
able rates. Is it true? Are the pressures worse today than in the past? If so,
why? Why now?

Recent trends in the Catholic priesthood will help us understand present-
day conditions. In the year 2001, we are thirty-six years past the close of the
Second Vatican Council, the most momentous change in Catholicism for many
centuries. The state of the Church today can be understood only from the seis-
mic shocks of the council and the events in subsequent years. Observers have
often noted that the council dealt with bishops, religious communities, and
the laity, but only tangentially with the priesthood. In the council's delibera-
tions, the priesthood was more a recipient of the innovations than their well-
spring—more a matter of being acted upon than being an actor.

In the years after the council, the Church changed in numerous ways,
some of which were entirely unforeseen. One of the most consequential
was a sharp decline in the number of men entering Catholic seminaries.
Seminaries in the United States were no exception. Since the late 1960s
they have suffered a long-term decline in enrollment. Priestly ordinations
dropped from 771 in 1975 to 533 in 1985, 511 in 1995, and 442 in 2000. The
slide was roughly 7% per decade in the 1980s and 1990s. It was more pre-
cipitous for religious ordinations (to orders and communities) than for diocesan ordinations. Nobody knows if the decline will continue, but we should
be skeptical about assertions heard occasionally that a trend so thoroughgoing has now been reversed. Possibly it is decelerating, but available data
are not clear enough that we can be sure.

In the year 2000 there were 30,607 diocesan priests and 15,092 religious priests in the United States, a total of 45,699. This compares with

1

57,317 in 1985, or a decline of about 13% per decade. The ranks of religious priests are thinning faster than those of diocesan priests—about 20% per decade. In 2000 the mean age of diocesan priests was 59, while that of religious priests was 63.

Over the postconciliar years the number of Catholics in the United States has risen; precise numbers are unavailable, but the best guess is that it continues to do so at about 8% to 12% per decade. The total in 2000 was about 61 or 62 million. The level of wealth among Catholics is also going up, so annual giving is greater than it has ever been, and endowments of parishes, hospitals, and universities are the highest in history.

The number of parishes has not changed for about twenty years; hence the average parish has grown about 10% per decade and will continue to grow. In 2000 the average parish had 3,086 members.

The priest-to-laity ratio in the year 2000 stood at 1:1,257, up from 1:652 in 1950, but it is interesting that it was higher in 1900, 1:899. Accordingly, we cannot look at 1950 as some kind of definition of "normality." The 1950s, commonly seen as the golden age of the pre-Vatican Council Church, enjoyed a larger than average number of seminarians, but since then the flow has greatly fallen off.

New ordinations are not nearly numerous enough to keep the priesthood at a stable size. Our best estimate is that ordinations in the past few years stand at approximately 35% of replacement level, that is, for every 1,000 priests dying, retiring, or resigning from the active priesthood, only about 350 new ones are being ordained. Clearly, the parish as we have known it cannot continue to be maintained.[1]

Has the rate of resignations changed recently? We know from past research that the priesthood experienced a bulge of resignations in the years 1968 to 1972; then the rate subsided and remained lower for many years. Since the middle 1980s it has increased.[2] The exact resignation rate today is unknown, but Sister Katarina Schuth, author of an important book on seminaries (1999), believes, on the basis of visits and interviews, that the figure is about 15%. This is guesswork, a bit higher figure than if we projected forward the trends

---

[1] The 35% estimate is based on data compiled by Richard Schoenherr and Lawrence Young (1993). I am confident that the true figure would fall between 30 and 40.

[2] We commissioned William P. Daly of the National Association of Church Personnel Administrators to gather resignation data for the 1970s, 1980s, and 1990s. He wrote to a random sample of 87 dioceses and orders and received information from 51. The percentage of new diocesan ordinands who resigned within five years was 5.5% for ordination years 1970–79, 5.1% for 1980–84, 7.3% for 1985–89, and 9.0% for 1990–94. For religious ordinands the figures were 5.1% for 1970–79, 4.3% for 1980–84, 5.7% for 1985–89, and 8.1% for 1990–94. See Daly (2001). Observers guess that the rate was higher since 1994, but we lack definite data.

since 1980. Projecting current trends would predict a resignation of about 10% or 12%. These resignations only worsen the priest shortage today.

Catholic parishes are large institutions, far too complex to be run by volunteers. Paid professionals are needed nowadays to do what priests did earlier, hence the dramatic 35% increase in professional lay ministers in a five-year period, from 21,569 in 1992 to an estimated 29,146 in 1997 (Murnion and DeLambo, 1999). A 1997 survey estimated that 27,000 priests are serving in parishes. In short, professional lay ministers are quickly filling in for priests in parish leadership, and already they outnumber the priests. In 1997 Murnion and DeLambo found that of the non-priest professional ministers, 71% are lay, 29% are vowed religious, and 82% are female. Parish leadership in the future will be different from anything Catholics have experienced in the past.

The New Priests

Are today's new priests different? Many observers have said that a certain percentage of the new priests are homosexual in orientation. No exact data are available, but persons who know the situation estimate that about one-fourth to one-half of the priests today have a homosexual orientation. How many are active? Everyone agrees it is a minority, but no one has exact information.[3] The urgent question before us is not how to get precise data but how best to manage seminaries and parishes in view of this situation. One difficulty is that a separate gay subcommunity could develop in seminaries or dioceses, and that could possibly be divisive.[4]

The age of seminarians has risen gradually over the last quarter century. Today the average age at ordination is 36; in 1984 it was 32. A similar circumstance obtains for Protestant seminarians.

How about the quality of seminarians in academic or leadership skills? Again, no scientific studies exist, but observers agree that academic quality has dropped gradually over the years, as it has in Protestant seminaries (Wheeler, 2001).

An additional new development is important. Seminary faculty report a growing polarization of students along ideological lines. The main battlegrounds are the nature of the priesthood, liturgy, devotions, and adherence to

---

[3] For the sake of readability we do not reference the many research studies here. Rather, the section "Additional Resources" after the Appendix lists the most important.

[4] Sulpician Father Melvin Blanchette and Sister Katarina Schuth, both researchers on seminarians and priests, agree that the resignation rate of homosexual priests is lower than that of heterosexuals. They base this conclusion on observations and interviews, not systematic research, since no research exists. This is an important topic which merits careful study. If more heterosexual priests resign after ordination, it raises the question of whether heterosexual seminarians more often drop out also prior to ordination.

orthodoxy (Schuth, 1999:78). A portion of Catholic seminarians today are firm in their loyalty to Pope John Paul II, their adherence to all Church teachings about sexual morality and contraception, and their preference for tradition and formality in ritual and priestly roles. They feel comfortable wearing cassocks in public, unlike the vast majority of priests two or three decades ago.

The polarization of seminarians extends to the priesthood; there is more polarization among priests today than there was twenty years ago. We have heard many reports of older priests being aghast at newly ordained priests who insisted on clear adherence to all Church rules and teachings; the former thought that insistence on many of the pre-Vatican Council rules was counterproductive with today's laity. Some of the newly ordained returned the criticism, saying that the older priests were sellouts to the culture and lacking in strong faith.

Changes in Culture

A research effort to explain changes in the experiences of priests over the past two or three decades must encompass analysis of cultural changes in the country. There have been many changes, and a goodly number have been measured and documented. Some examples: the average age at marriage has risen by more than three years since 1970; the number of persons cohabiting has gone up fivefold; international travel has become commonplace; attitudes toward premarital sex and homosexuality have become more liberal, and so on (Farley, 1996; Putnam, 2000).

Measuring cultural change is interesting, but the pertinent point here is which trends have impacted the lives of Catholic priests? Has the average age at marriage affected priests? Has the increase in computer and Internet use? Answers to questions such as these resist absolute proof, and we are left in the realm of guessing.

Guesses may be useful even if they aren't definitive. We postulate that three cultural trends *have* caused changes in the lives of priests. The first is the desire of American lay Catholics for more participatory Church structures. This trend has occurred mostly among younger Catholics, and it has been well documented (D'Antonio et al., 2001). Young Catholics, especially educated young Catholics, prefer Church governance to include more input from laypersons and even favor new procedures such as lay selection of priests for parishes. This trend has the effect of leveling the clergy-lay distinction in the minds of many Catholics, lessening the deference between laypersons and priests.

Second, religious authority is gradually being seen more and more as an individual matter rather than an institutional matter. The authority that Americans accorded the clergy and Church leaders in the past—the belief that the clergy really can be counted on to know the mind of God—has been gradually weakening, so priests today find that they need to earn that authority by their leadership and example; it does not come automatically with the office.

Third, attitudes in the realm of sexuality have liberalized, especially in regard to premarital sex and cohabitation. Young Americans are much more tolerant and individualistic on these matters than older persons, Catholic or not. The problem this raises for priests is that popular culture is gradually moving further and further away from Catholic moral teachings, making pastoral work more difficult.

Other analysts may make other guesses, and it is difficult to know how accurate such guesses are.

Research on Priestly Motivation and Resignations

We are not the first to look into priestly motivation and resignations. We know of at least a dozen studies, some on priestly motivation and some on resignations, done over the past thirty years. Here we will make a few summary statements. We will look first at research on motivation, then on resignations. At the beginning we need to recall a landmark 1970 study that looked at both. Carried out by Andrew Greeley and associates, its report was *The Catholic Priest in the United States: Sociological Investigations* (1972a). Greeley and associates surveyed a random sample of priests and every locatable resigned priest (men who resigned between 1965 and 1969). They found that the resigned priests were younger than average; the average age at resignation was about 35 for diocesan priests and 37 for religious (p. 24). The two main reasons for resignation were inability to live within the present institutional structure of the Church and the desire to marry. The resignees were distinctive in that they held ecclesiological attitudes that were more participatory and democratic than those of other priests of the same age. For example, the questionnaire asked for agreement or disagreement with the statement "I think it would be a good idea if Christian communities such as parishes were to choose their own priest from among available ordained priests." Of the resigned diocesan priests, 69% agreed, compared with 30% of active diocesan priests (p. 85).

Would the resigned priests like to return if they could do so as married priests? Thirty-six percent said they would "definitely like to return to work as a priest under certain conditions." A much smaller percentage were interested in returning to full-time ministry (p. 292).[5]

---

[5] Two large studies tried to assess organizational factors influencing the rates of priestly resignations. Schoenherr and Greeley (1974) looked at numerous factors but found practically no structural effects. Seidler (1979) found several predictors of resignation rates: percentage of parishes staffed by religious clergy, percentage of priests in nonparish work, and small Catholic population in the area. The theoretical meaning of these correlates was unclear.

Several studies of priestly morale and stress have been done in the past two decades. In 1990 a nationwide survey was undertaken of priests five to nine years after ordination to ascertain their opinions about seminary life and the transition to priesthood (Hemrick and Hoge, 1991). By using the same measures as in the landmark 1970 Greeley survey, the investigators assessed whether morale among recently ordained priests had gone up or down since 1970. It had gone up a modest amount. Why? Possibly because the resignations in the late 1980s had removed the most unhappy men from the priesthood, leaving a more contented remnant for the survey. Or possibly 1970 (the year of the earlier survey) had been a particularly bad year. The researchers had no way to know.

In 1999 NOCERCC, the National Organization for Continuing Education of Roman Catholic Clergy, commissioned a review of research on newly ordained priests, a review done by the present author (Hoge, 1999). The report summarized the main findings of five research studies done between 1984 and 1993. It concluded that newly ordained priests are as happy and fulfilled as other American men their age, and we should not see them as suffering from unusually bad morale problems. Yet they faced three important kinds of problems. First, their main stressor today is overwork and overresponsibility. Many young priests feel overwhelmed, and they lack the time to do the high-quality ministry they aspire to. Often they feel inadequately supervised. Their tasks require several specific skills in which many believe themselves deficient, which they identified as administration, management, finances, staff relationships, and conflict resolution.

Second, living arrangements are a problem. Many young priests find rectory or community living to be unsatisfactory, especially if they were assigned to their places of living. They would prefer to live in self-chosen groups, either in rectories, religious communities, or outside.

Third, some are unhappy with the diocesan structure. A good number feel left out of diocesan communications and decision-making. They have a sense of powerlessness and of being unappreciated.

A truth-speaking book by David K. O'Rourke, *The First Year of Priesthood* (1978), is the best single analysis of the transition to priesthood we know of. O'Rourke emphasizes problems in rectory living and in relations between newly ordained and senior pastors. He recommends a program that provides each beginning priest with a preceptor outside the parish.

The most incisive study of how priests think about problems in living a priestly life is Raymond Hedin's *Married to the Church* (1995). Hedin himself attended diocesan seminaries for nine years before dropping out in 1966. Years later he talked with many members of his class, including some thoughtful active priests. The latter told how they worry about money and how they feel bitter that they must scrimp and save, with no chance to live the same lifestyle as their parishioners.

Another subject they discussed was the celibacy requirement, which elicited a variety of interpretations. Some priests did not consider it binding. They saw it as a noble ideal but, in practice, no more than optional, and several told of long-term committed sexual relationships with women (p. 83). For these priests, celibacy was not a problem.

At the level of concrete action, the best work we know of on how to improve priestly morale appeared in *Origins:* "Reflections on the Morale of Priests" (NCCB, 1989). Written by a committee of parish priests, it recommends giving priests more voice in diocesan policies, having vicars for clergy elected by priests in each diocese, providing mentors for recently ordained priests, setting up adequate retirement policies, and more contact between priests and ordinaries.

A similar statement, also written by a committee of priests, recently appeared in *America*. Written by Thomas Sweetser (2001), it analyzes pressures on priests today and makes recommendations to the bishops on how to help alleviate them.

On priestly resignations, a useful study was done in 1985. Joseph Shields and Mary Jeanne Verdieck surveyed administrators of men's religious communities, and they asked questions about other priests who have resigned. Why, in the opinion of the administrators, did some priests resign in the preceding years? Their perceptions are shown in Table 1.1.

Table 1.1
Main Reasons for Resigning as Perceived by Administrators of Men's Religious Communities

	Percent "Very Frequent" and "Frequent"
Administrators' Perceived Reasons for Resignations:	
Preference for marriage	69
Problems with celibacy	68
No personal fulfillment	63
Dissatisfaction with community life	61
Problems with authority	34
Disenchantment with direction of community	33
Psychological disturbance	24
Weak formation	23
Interest in different mode of apostolate	17
New appreciation of lay roles	16
Completion of professional training	6

Source: Shields and Verdieck (1985).

The Shields and Verdieck study is different from the 1970 Greeley study in that it is based on observations by administrators, not on self-reports by resigned priests. Its findings differ from the 1970 research in that they place marriage and celibacy first as a motivator and rate dissatisfaction with the Church institution or community as of lesser importance. Some of the reasons at the bottom of the table's list, such as "weak formation" and "completion of professional training," strike us as interpretations made by administrators and not intrinsic motivations that priests themselves would give for resigning. They are, in any case, ranked much lower by the administrators.

The consistency of findings in past research signals the unlikelihood that a new study of priests will discover something new and unique. *Not that much* has changed in twenty years. Yet, new research has clear value. Above all, it lets us check on the situation today to see what has and has not changed in twenty or thirty years. It gives us an idea if any of the policy measures undertaken in that time interval have had a discernible effect. Also, it gives Church leaders new and reliable information for tackling today's problems, for which old data cannot be relied on. And new research, if it uses incisive methods and reliable sampling, can be an improvement. We are not called upon to draw entirely new maps, as were Lewis and Clark, but to update and improve what was done earlier. Our study done in 2000 was unprecedented in its sampling and methods, and it produced several new findings.

Chapter 2

Attitudes of Newly Ordained Active and Resigned Priests

Research Method

To get the information we needed, we (1) mailed questionnaires to a sample of active priests who had been ordained in 1995 to 1999, (2) phoned as many resigned priests as possible who were ordained in 1992 or later, and (3) interviewed 27 active and resigned priests in person. Even though we were mainly interested in the first five years of priesthood, we needed to extend the eligibility of resigned priests so that we could get enough cases; therefore we included men who had been ordained as far back as 1992.

The mail survey of active priests was conducted in mid-2000. We first wrote to all dioceses and religious institutes requesting names, then randomly selected 44 dioceses and 44 religious institutes for the sample. We sent out two waves of questionnaires to random samples of priests ordained between 1995 and 1999 in those groups (365 to diocesan; 346 to religious). We received 261 replies from diocesan and 266 from religious priests, and we found out that the addresses of 5 diocesan and 9 religious priests were erroneous. The response rates were 71% for the diocesan priests and 76% for the religious priests, giving us good data.

The telephone survey of resigned priests was more troublesome. We asked all the dioceses and religious institutes to supply names, and the members of the National Federation of Priests' Councils also tried to get names. We bought advertisements in two Catholic magazines and made many phone calls to friends asking for their help. We received about 246 names of resignees thought to have been ordained in 1992 or later, but for most we lacked an address or phone number. We tried to find the men through phone and Internet searches, and we asked all the resignees we interviewed to help us locate others. After extended effort, we succeeded in interviewing 72 (57 diocesan, 15 religious), which was fewer than we had hoped for. Of the names we collected, 145 were unreachable, 20 did not meet the eligibility requirements (usually ordination before 1992), and 9 refused to be interviewed.

Do the 72 represent all the recently resigned priests, or are they a biased sample? We have no way of being sure. Our best guess is that the men who consented to be interviewed were less angry and less conflicted than average. A number of the men whom we located and asked for interviews appeared to be emotionally on edge and tended to refuse an interview or to be evasive about when we should call back to do the interview. Later, when we analyzed the data, we learned that the 72 interviewees had been ordained relatively early in the period under study, mostly in 1992, 1993, or 1994. This seems to have been the result not only of the longer time span these men had served after ordination (hence more opportunity to resign) but also of the longer time elapsed since resignation (hence a longer settling-down period for their feelings). These ideas are largely speculations, but they are consistent with what we do know.

Early in 2001 we began personal interviews. By April we had finished 14 confidential taped interviews with active priests and 12 with resigned priests. Also, we asked one resigned priest to write an essay about his experiences.

Findings

This chapter presents the findings of the surveys of active and resigned priests under ten headings: (1) background and description of sample members, (2) life prior to seminary and in seminary, (3) evaluation of the theologate, (4) experiences in the priesthood, (5) living situation, (6) sources of satisfaction, (7) problems that priests face, (8) attitudes about the priesthood and the Church, (9) the decision to resign, and (10) occupations and plans of resigned priests.

1. Background and Description of Sample Members

Table 2.1 shows the data for active diocesan priests, active religious priests, and resigned priests. (For more detail, see Table A1 in the Appendix.) The average ages of the three sample members when surveyed were 40, 40, and 38. The resigned priests had been ordained at an earlier age than the active priests—an average of 32, compared with 36 for the active diocesan and 37 for the active religious priests. Their average age when resigning was 36, and their average period of service was four years.

Table 2.1
Background and Description of Sample Members

Number of cases:	Active Diocesan Priests (255) (%)	Active Religious Priests (256) (%)	Resigned Priests (72) (%)
Present age:			
29 or less	6	2	1
30–34	31	21	24
35–39	26	36	51
40–49	23	30	19
50–59	9	8	1
60 or more	5	3	3
In what year were you ordained?			
1992	0	0	35
1993	0	0	15
1994	0	0	18
1995	17	19	11
1996	23	17	8
1997	21	20	4
1998	21	21	7
1999	17	22	1
What was your age when you were ordained?			
Mean age	36	37	32
What was your age when you resigned?			
Mean age			36
Country of birth:			
United States	80	80	96
Other	20	20	4
What best describes your main racial or ethnic background?			
English, Irish, Scotch, Welsh	35	29	32
Western European	29	32	42
Eastern European	7	7	15
Hispanic	9	12	3
Black American	0	1	0
African	1	0	0
Asian	6	8	0
Filipino	2	2	1
Mixed or other	10	8	7

The resigned priests had been ordained a bit earlier than the active priests. Many were ordained in 1992 or 1993.[1]

Eighty percent of the recently ordained active priests were born in the United States. The second most common nation of birth was Vietnam. By contrast, 96% of the resignees were born in the United States, and the rest in the Philippines or Latin America. The resignees, then, were disproportionately U.S.-born. Of the priests born outside the United States, most had been here 15 years or more.

The vast majority of the newly ordained priests were of European ethnic background: 71% of the diocesan and 68% of the religious. The resigned priests were more commonly European, 89%, than the actives. Hispanics made up 9% of the recently ordained diocesan priests, 12% of the religious. Asians (including Filipinos) made up 8% of the recently ordained diocesan priests, 10% of the religious.

How many of these priests were converts to Catholicism? Not many. Of the active diocesan priests, 6%; of the active religious, 5%; of the resigned, 7%.

2. Life Prior to Seminary and in Seminary

When we began the project, we were told that many recently ordained priests had been inspired to enter seminary by an experience of spiritual awakening and that these priests were probably different from others. Accordingly, we asked our sample if this had been the case and if it was important in deciding upon their vocation. The majority said yes to both questions. The experiences mostly occurred between 15 and 24 years of age. Active and resigned priests were no different in the frequency of such experiences. (See Table 2.2.)

About half of the priests had attended seminary college before beginning theological studies: 50% of the active diocesan and 31% of the active religious. The resignees were similar: 46%. Also, the resignees resembled the actives in that they had worked full-time for a year or more before theological studies: 76% of the active diocesan, 80% of the active religious, and 71% of the resignees. The only difference was that the resignees had

---

[1] Because the active priests had, on average, fewer years of service, it is possible that the comparison between them and the resigned priests is biased. Possibly priests in the first year or two are in a "honeymoon" period. To check, we compared the total sample of active priests with the subsample of those ordained in 1995, 1996, and 1997. This allowed us to estimate if the priests ordained in the last two years were different. We found no systematic differences, so the total sample of ordinands from 1995 to 1999 can represent the ordinands ordained from 1995 to 1997.

worked for a shorter time. In all three samples, the most common occupations prior to theological study were business management, teaching, sales, and clerical.

Table 2.2
Life Prior to Seminary and in Seminary

	Active Diocesan Priests (%)	Active Religious Priests (%)	Resigned Priests (%)
Did you have an experience of spiritual awakening in your youth or adult years?			
Yes, and it was important for my vocation.	66	64	60
Yes, but it was not important for my vocation.	13	9	8
No	21	27	32
Before beginning theological studies, did you attend seminary college?			
Yes	50	31	46
No	50	69	54
Before beginning theological studies in the seminary, did you work full-time for a year or more?			
Yes	76	80	71
No	24	20	29
If yes, for how many years?			
1–4 years	36	39	62
5 or more years	64	61	38
Did you take time out from studies during your theological seminary years?			
Yes	18	16	21
No	82	84	79

The undergraduate major courses of all three samples were similar; most common were humanities, social sciences, and business. The total number of years of seminary training was also similar in the three samples. (For details, see Table A1 in the Appendix.)

Did these priests take time out from studies during their theological seminary years? Not many did. Of the active diocesan, only 18% had done so; of the active religious, 16%; and of the resigned, 21%.

We collected all this information to see if it predicted resignations from the priesthood later. None had much predictive power.

3. Evaluation of the Theologate

Table 2.3 depicts the priests' ratings of fourteen aspects of their theological training (for details, see the Appendix). Overall the ratings were positive. Specifically, the respondents rated four aspects *very favorably,* with little difference among the three samples: formal theological training, homiletics, spirituality and prayer life, and pastoral care and counseling.

Table 2.3

How Well Did Your Theologate Prepare You in These Areas?

(Percent saying "Very well" or "Well," in descending order)

	Active Diocesan Priests (%)	Active Religious Priests (%)	Resigned Priests (%)
Formal theological training	95	98	97
Homiletics	88	86	91
Pastoral care and counseling	87	83	82
Understanding yourself as a sexual person	81	72	51
Balancing self-care and ministry	79	65	74
Spirituality and prayer life	77	77	89
Understanding changes in the priesthood	75	68	61
Developing personal support networks	72	66	57
Handling multiple tasks and responsibilities	69	62	62
Working with lay staff	66	68	61
Working with multiple ethnic groups	63	64	66
Handling problems of loneliness	63	48	38
Church administration	28	19	24
(Religious only): Preparation for the religious life		31	

The priests rated four aspects *somewhat favorably,* again with little difference among the three samples: balancing self-care and ministry; working with lay staff; handling multiple tasks and responsibilities; and working with multiple ethnic groups.

They rated one topic *very unfavorably:* church administration, again with little difference among the samples. This aspect had by far the lowest rating.

On four aspects the three samples disagreed, with the resigned consistently making lower ratings. The four, in order of the size of the gap between active diocesan and resigned priests, were: (1) Understanding yourself as a sexual person. The resigned priests rated their theologates much lower. The gap between active diocesan and resigned priests was 30 percentage points. (2) Handling problems of loneliness. The active priests gave their theologates moderate ratings, while the resigned priests gave them low ratings. The gap between the active diocesan and resigned priests was 25 percentage points. (3) Developing personal support networks. The spread between active diocesan and resignees was 15 percentage points. (4) Understanding changes in the priesthood. The spread between active diocesan and resignees was 14 percentage points. These four aspects, taken together, give us a clue as to the feelings of alienation among the resigned priests.

In sum, the resigned priests were especially critical of their theological training in one domain, that of *preparing them for the celibate life and for coping with problems of loneliness.*

4. Experiences in the Priesthood

We tested several more hypotheses about who resigns. First, we had been told that priests who resigned had been serving farther away from their childhood home than others and possibly had suffered greater loneliness. We asked both diocesan and religious priests about this and found that active and resigned priests were not different: the priests who resigned had served just as close to their childhood homes as others.

Second, we hypothesized that priests who resigned had been serving in relatively larger dioceses. This turned out to be true. Forty-four percent of the resigned diocesan priests had been in dioceses of 200 priests or more, compared with 32% of the active diocesan priests. The same was true of the resigned religious priests: they had been in larger provinces (although our conclusion must be tentative in light of the small number of cases in our sample). Possibly larger dioceses and provinces provide less personal attention to newly ordained priests.

How favorable were the experiences of these priests in their first assignments? For the active priests, good; for the resigned priests, mediocre. We asked, "How would you rate your first assignment after ordination in terms of helping you make the transition from seminary to priestly ministry?" (see Table 2.4). Seventy-eight percent of the active diocesan priests said "very helpful" or "helpful," compared with 74% of the religious priests and only 47% of the resigned priests.

Table 2.4
Experiences in the Priesthood

	Active Diocesan Priests (%)	Active Religious Priests (%)	Resigned Priests (%)
How would you rate your first assignment after ordination in terms of helping you make the transition from seminary to priestly ministry?			
Very helpful	46	42	24
Helpful	32	32	23
Not too helpful	12	22	31
Detrimental	10	4	22
Why was it helpful or not helpful? (up to 2 ideas coded)			
Positive:			
Supportive, understanding pastor	44	13	22
Supportive parishioners	14	12	4
Supportive priests (other than pastor)	2	4	10
Good transition process	3	8	7
Good parish, active parish	7	7	7
Good pace of work, not overburdened	2	4	3
Could carry out my sacramental priestly role	3	10	1
Good opportunities, good fulfillment	12	18	5
Large parish	7	3	5
Small parish	1	1	0
Familiar setting	1	5	1
Negative:			
Unsupportive pastor, problem pastor	19	5	33
Unsupportive parishioners	0	0	3
Unsupportive priests (other than pastor)	0	2	3
Poor transition process	3	6	8
Few opportunities to carry out my sacramental priestly role	0	3	4
Few opportunities for fulfillment	0	3	3
No mentor; absence of pastor	1	3	1
Little privacy, too public, too much action	1	2	10
Different role than I was trained for	1	4	5
Other	2	1	1

Have you been involved in a formal mentoring program after ordination?

Yes	39	20	40
No	61	80	60

(If yes:) Was it helpful?

Very helpful	34	49	14
Helpful	41	42	38
Not too helpful	25	5	48
Detrimental	0	4	0

What is your current ministerial position?

Pastor	21	7
Parochial vicar	66	35
Full-time administration	3	7
Educational apostolate	3	28
Hospital or prison chaplaincy	1	1
Ministry with a special group	1	7
Other	4	15

Do you (or did you) have enough freedom and authority to make decisions in carrying out your ministry?

Yes	86	87	68
No	14	13	32

(If no:) Explain: (percents based on 37, 34, and 22 cases)

Pastor made all decisions	57	35	36
Pastor was easily threatened	11	9	18
Too functionary	3	3	9
Not part of planning process	11	17	4
Could only make suggestions	5	15	18
All decisions were made by religious community	5	12	5
Other	8	9	9

Why was the experience good or bad? The priests whose experiences were good cited supportive pastors, supportive parishioners, and good opportunities for personal fulfillment. The priests with bad experiences cited unsupportive pastors, a poor transition process, and inadequate opportunities for a sacramental priestly role or for personal fulfillment. Also, the dissatisfied priests cited too little privacy and having too public a life.

As we might expect, the resigned priests had the most complaints about their first assignment. Their main grievances were having an unsupportive pastor and too little privacy.

We wondered if the resigned priests had been involved less frequently in a formal mentoring program after graduation. We asked and found no difference: the active and resigned priests had had the same amount of involvement. Did both groups of priests find the mentoring experience to be equally helpful? No, the resigned priests rated it much lower. Among the active diocesan priests, 75% said the mentoring program had been "very helpful" or "helpful"; 91% of the active religious priests said this, and 52% of the resigned.

Were the priests satisfied or dissatisfied with the help and support they received from fellow priests, either older priests with more years of service or priests who had been ordained at about the same time? The majority of all the priests were satisfied on both counts, but the active priests had higher levels of satisfaction than the resigned.

Ministerial Position

We asked the active priests what position they currently held and found that 21% of the diocesan priests and 7% of the religious priests were pastors, even though they had been ordained an average of only three years. The vast majority of the diocesan priests, as we expected, were parochial vicars. Of the religious priests, 35% were parochial vicars, 28% were in educational apostolates, 7% were in ministries with a special group, and 15% said "other" (see Table 2.4).

Did these priests feel that they had enough freedom and authority to make decisions in carrying out their ministry? Yes; 86% of the diocesan and 87% of the religious priests said so. We asked the same question of the resigned priests concerning their last ministry, and only 68% said yes. If not, what was the problem? The major problems cited were all variations on a theme, variously expressed as "the pastor made all decisions," "was not part of the planning process," "could make suggestions only," or "the pastor was easily threatened." The problem was felt similarly by active and resigned priests, but more frequently by the latter.

5. Living Situation

Were the priests in our samples satisfied with their living situation in their first assignment? Most were. Saying "very satisfied" or "somewhat satisfied" were 73% of the active diocesan priests, 71% of the active religious, and 53% of the resigned priests. Probably their living situation had some influence on the decision of resigned priests to leave.

What caused the majority to be satisfied? They cited comfortable and ample space, personal privacy, and agreeable fellow priests. Many of the religious priests cited "good community life." Why did others express dissatisfaction? The main complaints were a lack of personal privacy, living quarters too close to their office, problems with the pastor or other priests, and poor community life. The resigned priests were not unique in what they complained about, but they made more complaints (see Table 2.5).

Were the active priests satisfied with their current living situations? Mostly yes: 60% of the diocesan and 45% of the religious priests were "very satisfied." Only 15% of the diocesan and 18% of the religious said they were "somewhat dissatisfied" or "very dissatisfied." Their reasons for satisfaction or dissatisfaction were similar to their reasons relative to their first assignment. Indeed, many are still in their first assignment now.

Were these priests satisfied with the help and support they receive from priests with more years of service? (In interviews with resigned priests, the same question was asked, but regarding their last assignment.) Most were "very satisfied" or "somewhat satisfied": 81% of the diocesan, 76% of the religious, and 57% of the resigned. Yet, a few were unhappy; 5% of the diocesan, 6% of the religious, and 17% of the resigned said "very dissatisfied." (For more detail, see Table A7 in the Appendix.)

How about the support from other priests in their diocese or community who were ordained at about the same time? The responses were similar: 77% of the diocesan, 72% of the religious, and 54% of the resigned said "very satisfied" or "somewhat satisfied." Five percent of the diocesan, 7% of the religious, and 19% of the resigned said "very dissatisfied." Here is another factor that figured in some priests' resignations. In a survey such as ours, we cannot discern the *source* of the cold relationships some priests experienced with other priests. We have no idea who or what it may have been. It is possible that the absence of supportive bonds with other priests resulted from the actions of the new priests themselves.

6. Sources of Satisfaction

We asked a general question about the satisfactions of being a priest: "There are many sources of satisfaction in the life and work of a priest. How important is each of the following [nine possible sources] *as a source of satisfaction to you?*" (See Table 2.6; for details, see Table A4 in the Appendix.) The resigned priests answered the same question, but in respect to their lives when they were still active. The question turned out to be useful for identifying the main satisfactions of newly ordained priests today, but not for distinguishing active priests from resigned priests. All the samples gave similar responses, agreeing on what gave them the most satisfaction as priests.

Table 2.5
Satisfaction with Living Situation

	Active Diocesan Priests (%)	Active Religious Priests (%)	Resigned Priests (%)
Were you satisfied or dissatisfied with your living situation in your first assignment?			
Very satisfied	49	41	18
Somewhat satisfied	24	30	35
Somewhat dissatisfied	11	13	21
Very dissatisfied	15	15	25
Don't know, or other	1	1	1
Why were you satisfied or dissatisfied?			
Positive:			
Personal privacy	8	2	6
Living quarters separate from office	3	3	0
Comfortable space, ample	14	3	8
Had practical needs met	3	3	4
Liked urban environment	1	2	0
Agreeable priests, pastor	18	8	7
Had own home, apartment	3	0	1
Good community life	3	31	11
Negative:			
Living quarters inadequate	3	1	1
Lack of personal privacy	12	3	14
Living quarters too close to office	6	1	13
Problems with priests, pastor	11	16	15
Felt like guest in pastor's house	3	2	7
Lack of community life	2	10	7
Didn't like community life	1	4	1
Church, community too small	0	3	0
Other	9	7	3
Are you satisfied or dissatisfied with your living situation now?			
Very satisfied	60	45	
Somewhat satisfied	23	35	
Somewhat dissatisfied	8	12	
Very dissatisfied	7	6	
Don't know, or other	2	2	
Why are you satisfied or dissatisfied?			
Positive:			
Personal privacy	8	5	
Living quarters separate from office	6	2	
Comfortable space	11	3	

Ample quarters	7	1
Have practical needs met	4	6
Agreeable priests, pastor	16	6
Have own home, apartment	9	3
Good community life	5	30
Negative:		
Living quarters inadequate	1	1
Lack of personal privacy	6	4
Living quarters too close to office	5	2
Problems with priests, pastor	8	12
Felt like guest in pastor's house	2	0
Lack of community life	3	7
Didn't like community life	1	2
Church, community too small	0	3
Other	8	14

Table 2.6
Nine Sources of Satisfaction for Priests
(Percent saying "Of great importance," in descending order)

	Active Diocesan Priests (%)	Active Religious Priests (%)	Resigned Priests (%)
Administering the sacraments and presiding over the liturgy	97	92	85
Preaching the Word	89	87	90
Helping people and families in their daily lives	79	76	82
The opportunity to work with many people and be a part of their lives	75	74	82
Security that your vocation is a response to the divine call	72	54	47
Being a visible sign of the Catholic Church	54	47	28
Administering the life of the Church	46	30	35
Being respected as a leader of Christians	37	28	35
Living the common life with like-minded priests or members of your religious community	27	62	26

Clearly the greatest satisfactions for priests come from what might be called the "big three": administering the sacraments, presiding over the liturgy, and preaching the Word. Past research has found the same. These three are expressed in the top two items in the table. After them in importance come the satisfaction of helping people and families in their daily lives and the opportunity to be a part of many people's lives. Additional but somewhat weaker sources of satisfaction are the spiritual security of knowing that being a priest is a response to the divine call and the experience of being a visible public sign of the Catholic Church.

The differences between active and resigned priests are mostly small, yet they are large on two sources of satisfaction: "being a visible sign of the Catholic Church" (resigned were 26 percentage points lower than active diocesan priests) and "security that your vocation is a response to the divine call" (resigned were 25 percentage points lower). Here is an indication that the spiritual lives of the resigned priests were different from the lives of the active priests, or at least different as they remember today. The resigned priests did not experience the same personal rewards from the experience of representing the Church in public or from the assurance that they were answering God's call. Possibly they felt less deep satisfaction from their obedience to God and the Church.

We made a second attempt to assess satisfaction by using more concrete questions. We asked the active priests, "At present, what is your level of satisfaction with the following [ten items]?" and asked the resigned priests the same about their last priestly position (see Table 2.7).

At this more concrete level, we discovered sizeable differences between active and resigned priests. The greatest by far was in "living a celibate life." Whereas 53% of the active diocesan priests and 33% of the active religious priests said they were "very satisfied," only 7% of the resigned priests said the same. Moreover, 42% of the resigned priests said they had been "very dissatisfied," compared with 4% of the active diocesan and 7% of the religious. Here is a major reason that many of the priests resigned. A question remains: Why did some priests find celibacy so troublesome and other priests not? Does the explanation lie in the number with a homosexual orientation? Differences in sex drive? Differences in susceptibility to loneliness? Our survey yields no information. We return to this question, a key to understanding priestly satisfaction or dissatisfaction, in Chapter 4.

The resigned priests were different from active priests in other ways too. Fewer said they were satisfied with their living situation (34 percent lower than active diocesan priests), their work in ministry (29 points lower), and their relationship with their bishop or superior (26 points lower). The active and resigned gave similar ratings to several sources of satisfaction: relationships with laity, fairness and openness in chancery decisions, spiritual life, and opportunities for continuing education.

Table 2.7
"What is Your Level of Satisfaction with the Following?"
(Percent saying "Very satisfied," in descending order)

	Active Diocesan Priests (%)	Active Religious Priests (%)	Resigned Priests (%)
Your relationship with the laity with whom you work	73	67	67
Current work in ministry	72	61	43
Your living situation	58	46	24
Living a celibate life	53	33	7
Your relationship with the bishop or superior	48	44	22
The support you receive from fellow priests	39	30	19
Spiritual life	31	26	21
Opportunities for continuing education	28	32	26
Personal time schedule	26	18	14
Fairness and openness in chancery decisions	24	25	14

Another lesson seen in the table should be mentioned: priests are more satisfied with their relationships with laity than with relationships with fellow priests, bishops, or superiors.

Figure 2.1 illustrates the differences between active and resigned priests. In it the category "active priests" comprises both diocesan and religious (80% diocesan and 20% religious, their actual proportions among the newly ordained). Here we can begin to identify the main sources of satisfaction that sustain active priests and the main sources of dissatisfaction that lead some priests to resign soon after ordination. The active priests find great satisfaction in relations with laity and current work in ministry. The resigned priests found celibacy, living situations, and relationships with bishops or superiors to be alienating. The active and the resigned *agreed* that relationships with the laity were highly satisfying to all.

Figure 2.1
"What is Your Level of Satisfaction with the Following?"
(Percent "Very Satisfied")

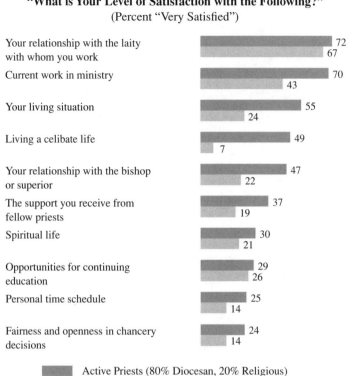

Your relationship with the laity
with whom you work — 72 / 67

Current work in ministry — 70 / 43

Your living situation — 55 / 24

Living a celibate life — 49 / 7

Your relationship with the bishop
or superior — 47 / 22

The support you receive from
fellow priests — 37 / 19

Spiritual life — 30 / 21

Opportunities for continuing
education — 29 / 26

Personal time schedule — 25 / 14

Fairness and openness in chancery
decisions — 24 / 14

■ Active Priests (80% Diocesan, 20% Religious)
■ Resigned Priests

7. Problems That Priests Face

We prefaced a series of fifteen questions with a statement: "Priests face many problems today. Would you indicate how important the following problems are *to you* on a day-to-day basis?" Table 2.8 shows the percentages of diocesan, religious, and resigned priests who said of each item that it was "a great problem to me." (The other possible responses: "somewhat of a problem," "very little problem," and "no problem.") When interviewing the resigned priests, we asked them about how important the problems "*were* to you."

Table 2.8 is a useful depiction of the main problems facing newly ordained priests. The top four for resigned priests are "living a celibate life," "loneliness of priestly life," "difficulty of establishing private living space," and "the way authority is too heavy-handed in the Church." For diocesan priests the top four are "too much work," "disagreement with other priests over ecclesiology and ministry," "difficulty of establishing private living space," and "unrealistic demands and expectations of lay people." The top four for religious priests are "too much work," "loneliness of priestly life," "the way authority is too heavy-handed in the Church," and "living a celibate life." All these deserve the attention of Church leaders.

Table 2.8
Problems that Face Priests Today
(Percent saying "A great problem," in descending order)

	Active Diocesan Priests (%)	Active Religious Priests (%)	Resigned Priests (%)
Living a celibate life	7	13	47
Loneliness of priestly life	8	18	46
Difficulty of establishing private living space	10	9	36
The way authority is too heavy-handed in the Church	3	16	34
Being a public person all the time	9	11	31
Too much work	13	24	28
Unrealistic demands and expectations of lay people	10	9	24
Being expected to represent Church teachings you have difficulty with	4	12	22
Disagreement with other priests over ecclesiology and ministry	12	9	21
Your relationship with your pastor	8	6	18
Lack of agreement on what a priest is	8	7	17
Your relationship with your bishop or major superior	2	3	14
Inadequate salary and benefits	7	4	11
Difficulty of really reaching people today	5	5	7
The way authority is too lax in the Church	6	2	4

The active religious priests, to our surprise, are more troubled by loneliness than are diocesan priests. We expected the opposite, because the former commonly live in communities, not alone or in small rectories. Also to our surprise, the religious priests are more troubled by "heavy-handed authority" in the Church than are diocesan priests. Why? We expected the opposite, theorizing that religious priests are less impacted by Church authority. Possibly the diocesan and religious priesthoods attract different personality types or have different training, for we have not uncovered any organizational reason for the differing responses.

Figure 2.2 illustrates the large gap between active and resigned priests on the problems at issue.

Figure 2.2
"Priests Face Many Problems. How Important Are (Were) the Following Problems to You on a Day-To-Day Basis?"
(Percent "A Great Problem to Me")

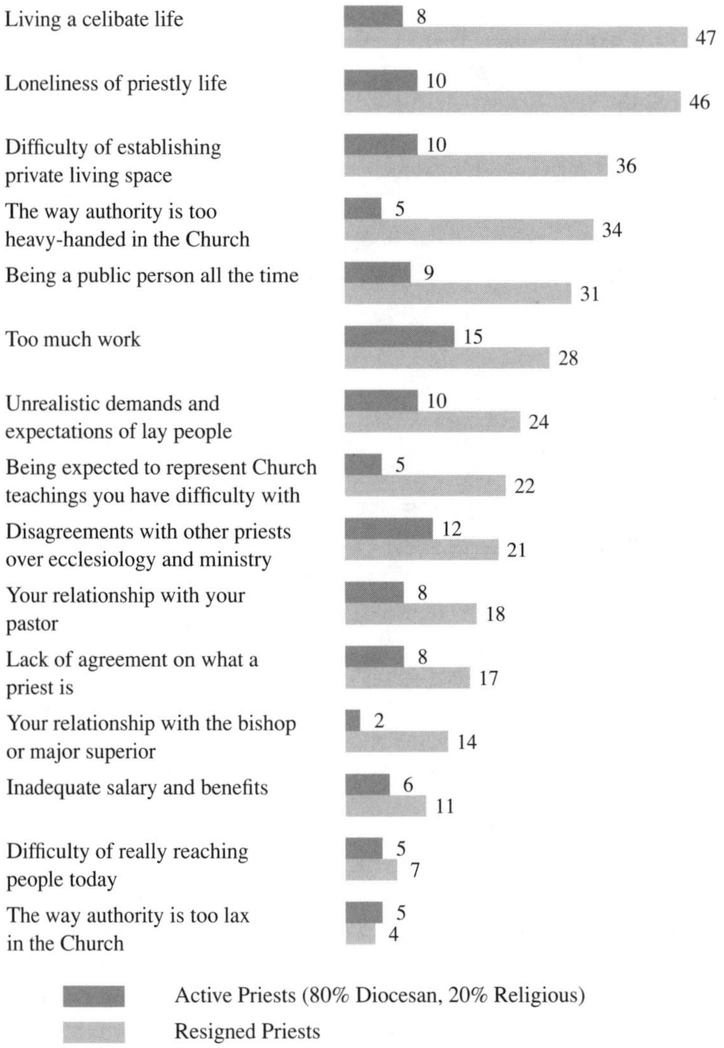

Problem	Active	Resigned
Living a celibate life	8	47
Loneliness of priestly life	10	46
Difficulty of establishing private living space	10	36
The way authority is too heavy-handed in the Church	5	34
Being a public person all the time	9	31
Too much work	15	28
Unrealistic demands and expectations of lay people	10	24
Being expected to represent Church teachings you have difficulty with	5	22
Disagreements with other priests over ecclesiology and ministry	12	21
Your relationship with your pastor	8	18
Lack of agreement on what a priest is	8	17
Your relationship with the bishop or major superior	2	14
Inadequate salary and benefits	6	11
Difficulty of really reaching people today	5	7
The way authority is too lax in the Church	5	4

Active Priests (80% Diocesan, 20% Religious)
Resigned Priests

The resigned priests rated several problems as *much greater* than the active ones did: (1) They were 39 percentage points higher on saying that "living a celibate life" was a major problem. (2) They were 36 percentage points higher on "loneliness of priestly life." (3) They were 29 points higher on "the way authority is too heavy-handed in the Church." (4) They were 26 points higher on "difficulty of establishing private living space."

Two problems in Table 2.8 were written in a way that permitted us to compare the responses: "The way authority is too heavy-handed in the Church" and "The way authority is too lax in the Church." The results are instructive. The resigned priests were distinctive in their responses: 34% said that heavy-handed authority was a great problem, while only 4% said that laxness was a great problem. By contrast, the active diocesan priests saw *both* as unimportant, with only 6% and 3% respectively saying they are "a great problem." The religious priests' responses were between the other two samples. Sixteen percent said that heavy-handedness was a great problem, and 2% said the same about laxness; that is, heavy-handedness had been troublesome for many resigned priests and a modest number of religious priests, but not for many diocesan priests. We were surprised how different the diocesan priests were from the religious priests on this question. (We will see more evidence of differences below.)

8. Attitudes about the Priesthood and the Church

The Catholic clergy hold diverse opinions on many topics pertaining to the priesthood and Church governance. Ecclesiological debates may have been important to the newly ordained priests, so we wanted to find out their attitudes. We asked them if they agreed or disagreed with nine specific statements (see Table 2.9). (The available responses were "strongly agree," "moderately agree," "uncertain," "moderately disagree," and "strongly disagree.")

Table 2.9 displays surprisingly large differences among our three samples. The active diocesan priests were the most insistent that ordination confers on the priest a new status that makes him essentially different from the laity, that a priest should see himself as a "man set apart" by God, and that it is essential to emphasize the distinction between priests and laity. On the other hand, the resigned priests were by far the most favorably disposed toward letting celibacy be optional for diocesan priests, to expanding the ministries of women, and to giving priests more say in choosing their assignments and living arrangements.

The religious priests fell between the diocesan priests and the resigned priests on these topics. The gaps between diocesan and religious priests are sometimes large—for example, on optional celibacy, 35 percentage points, and on expansion of women's ministries, 30 percentage points. Figure 2.3 illustrates responses to the four statements on which the gaps are greatest.

Clearly the resigned priests are more innovation-minded regarding the priesthood than the active priests in general, and much more than the diocesan priests in particular.

Table 2.9
Agreement with Nine Statements About the Priesthood and the Church
(Percent agreeing strongly or moderately, listed in order of the difference between diocesan and resigned priests)

	Active Diocesan Priests (%)	Active Religious Priests (%)	Resigned Priests (%)	Diff- erence (%)
Celibacy should be an option for diocesan priests.	29	64	94	65
Ordination confers on the priest a new status which makes him essentially different from the laity.	75	52	27	48
The Catholic Church should allow women greater partici- pation in all ministries.	45	75	90	45
A priest must see himself as a "man set apart" by God.	69	40	28	41
It is essential to make the distinction between priests and laity more important in the Church.	43	24	8	35
Catholic laity need to be better educated to respect the author- ity of the priest's word.	36	16	9	27
Priests today should be given much more say in choosing their assignments.	50	59	75	25
Priests today should be given much more freedom to choose their living arrangements.	51	41	72	21
Priests today should be more involved with broad social issues.	74	84	89	15

Figure 2.3
Four Statements About Priesthood and Ministry on Which
Differences Are Greatest (in percents)

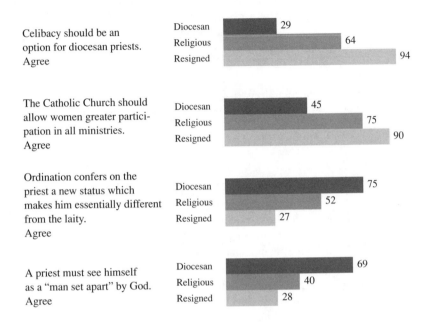

Celibacy should be an option for diocesan priests. Agree

Diocesan 29
Religious 64
Resigned 94

The Catholic Church should allow women greater participation in all ministries. Agree

Diocesan 45
Religious 75
Resigned 90

Ordination confers on the priest a new status which makes him essentially different from the laity. Agree

Diocesan 75
Religious 52
Resigned 27

A priest must see himself as a "man set apart" by God. Agree

Diocesan 69
Religious 40
Resigned 28

The great dissimilarities between diocesan priests' opinions and those of religious priests took us by surprise. It seems that the two have different ecclesiologies, stemming either from disparate themes in seminary training or from disparate types of persons who enter seminaries in the first place with intentions of becoming one type or the other.

Table 2.9 gives us valuable insights into the resigned priests. They were almost unanimous in favoring optional celibacy for diocesan priests, greater participation of women in all ministries, and more involvement by priests in broad social issues. They almost unanimously disagreed with two statements: "Catholic laity need to be better educated to respect the authority of the priest's word" and "It is essential to make the distinction between priests and laity more important in the Church." They strongly favored giving priests much more freedom to choose their living arrangements and their assignments. Did they have these attitudes when they resigned? Our best evidence from personal interviews is that they did, and that as priests they were already more participatory in their ecclesiology than average.

Suggestions for Preparing Seminarians and Priests

We asked the three samples an open-ended question: "What suggestions would you make to Catholic leadership to help them prepare seminarians and newly ordained priests more effectively for priestly ministry?" Some of the responses were long; we coded the two most important suggestions for each. (See Table 2.10.)

Table 2.10
Suggestions to Catholic Leadership
(Coded categories of open-ended suggestions, in percents)

	Active Diocesan Priests (%)	Active Religious Priests (%)	Resigned Priests (%)
Develop more administrative, management, and human relations skills	23	19	9
More practical training in seminary; require an internship or a time away from the seminary before ordination	20	17	32
More focus on prayer, spiritual formation, and on being a spiritual leader	18	21	7
Develop more counseling and pastoral care skills	6	8	11
More training on liturgy and preaching	7	4	2
More training on doctrine	6	5	1
More training on living a celibate life, sexuality, and intimacy	4	4	19
More training on working with laity, especially women	3	7	10
More open dialogue and honesty in seminary training	9	10	12
Deal better with personal problems before ordination	7	16	20
Seminarians should be less isolated	2	2	12
Plan first assignments better, with good pastors	4	2	8
Better formal mentoring and peer support programs	9	7	4
Other	9	8	4

From the responses it was apparent that the priests appreciated the opportunity to make recommendations, and they took the task seriously. Their ideas were diverse, and we categorized them in the entries in Table 2.10. Our categorization revealed several main themes: more practical experience, more on-the-job training, and more teaching of specific skills, including administration, prayer, and spiritual formation. The resigned priests more often suggested internships, better training in celibacy, and less isolation.

Homosexuality in the priesthood is a much discussed subject today, so we asked the resigned priests during the interview if they had any concerns about it. Forty-five persons voiced concerns, summarized in Table 2.11. The most common opinion was that the Church needs to deal openly with gay issues. About one-fifth of those voicing concerns said that the gay lifestyle in the priesthood seemed to be increasing.

Table 2.11
Concerns About Homosexuality Issues
(Coded responses to open-ended questions, in percents)

	Resigned Priests (%)
"What are your concerns, if any, about homosexuality issues in the priesthood?"	
The Church needs to deal more openly with gay issues.	49
More priests are homosexual than the public knows, and the priesthood is becoming homosexual.	20
Emphasize that being celibate is more important than whether a priest is heterosexual or homosexual.	17
Other	14

9. The Decision to Resign

When did the resignees first think seriously about leaving the priesthood? It is a complex question to ask in an interview, because in normal life, thoughts about all kinds of things arrive unbidden. Thus our question was really posed to ascertain when the resignee first thought *seriously* about leaving. The answer, of course, depends on one's judgment about seriousness. We found that 32% said they first thought seriously about it before ordination, that is, had grave misgivings about being ordained at all (Table 2.12).

Table 2.12
The Decision to Resign

	Active Diocesan Priests (%)	Active Religious Priests (%)	Resigned Priests (%)
When did you first think seriously about leaving the priesthood?			
Before ordination			32
After ordination			68
Which of the following statements reflects your feelings about your future in the priesthood?			
I definitely will not leave.	71	58	
I probably will not leave.	24	28	
I am uncertain about my future.	4	11	
I probably will leave.	1	2	
I have definitely decided to leave.	0	1	
What were your main motivations to resign? (up to 2 ideas coded)			
Fell in love; wanted marriage or intimate relationship with a woman			42
Celibacy was a problem			26
Dissatisfaction with church administration or trends			16
Loneliness was a problem			15
As a gay person, was not understood or supported			7
Left because of illness			7
Little room to express personal gifts or talents			7
Overwhelmed with demands of superiors			5
Overwhelmed with responsibilities toward parishioners			4
Discouragement with fellow priests			4
Discomfort with fellow priests			4
Other			8

What about the newly ordained active priests? Do many of them today have thoughts of resigning? Of the diocesan priests, 71% told us they definitely will not leave; 5% were uncertain or thinking about it more or less seriously. Among the religious priests, 58% told us they definitely will not leave; 14% were uncertain or thinking about it more or less seriously.

Why did the resignees leave? During the interview we asked them to try to judge what their main motivations were. They typically mentioned several, but we asked them to identify the main ones, and we coded up to two per interview (see Table 2.12).

The most common motive for resigning, in the resignees' accounts, was the desire to marry. Some were in love, others were not but had difficulties with celibacy. Two other motives were also important: dissatisfaction with Church leadership and the pains of loneliness. During the research we heard numerous stories of priests who fell in love, and the ones who subsequently resigned usually had felt dissatisfaction with the priesthood before they entered into the love relationship. Happy and fulfilled priests rarely resign, even if they find themselves in love. We concluded that more than one motivation is present in almost all cases of priestly resignations. Chapter 4 investigates this matter in more detail.

10. Occupations and Plans of Resigned Priests

What were the future plans of the resigned priests? What are they doing now? (See Table 2.13.)

The resigned priests hoped to be Christian ministers, social workers, business or finance professionals, teachers, or technical experts. Just now some are in temporary jobs, while others are earning graduate degrees or are enrolled in other training programs.

Currently, 35% of the resigned priests are married, and 4% are engaged or living in a committed relationship. If priests could be married, the majority (64%) would be interested in becoming an active married priest.

Did the resigned priests seek a dispensation? No, not the majority. Why not? The most common reasons given were that they thought a dispensation was theologically inappropriate; they saw no reason for it; or they didn't want to submit themselves to the Church's scrutiny or judgment. Several wanted to keep open the option of returning to the active priesthood.

Table 2.13
Occupations and Plans of Resigned Priests

	Percents
Long-range plan for future occupation	
Christian ministry (e.g., youth minister, chaplain)	18
Business management, finance, accounting	14
Social worker, counselor	18
Technician, mechanical, paramedical	4
Sales, clerical	3
Engineer, scientist, computers, professor	6
Teaching elementary or high school	6
Administration, assistant	3
Government, public service	1
Physician	4
Other	7
Don't know	17
Current marital status	
Married	35
Engaged or in a committed relationship	4
Single	61
If priests could be married, would you be interested in being an active married priest?	
Yes	64
No	28
Don't know	8
Do you consider yourself an active Catholic now?	
Yes	78
No	22
Since leaving the priesthood, have you tried to get a dispensation? Why or why not?	
Yes, I have applied and am waiting.	7
Yes, now thinking about it.	7
Yes, I want to be married in the Church.	6
No, it is theologically inappropriate.	17
No, there is no reason to do it.	14
No, I was told it won't be considered until I'm over age 40.	11
No, I don't want the Church's scrutiny or judgment.	11
No, I may still return to the priesthood.	8
No, other	19

Chapter 3

What Makes for
Satisfied Newly Ordained Priests?

We gathered a good random sample of priests ordained one to five years ago, who gave us reliable information on their situations and helped us identify those with a high or low level of satisfaction in their priesthood. As we have seen in Chapter 2, most were satisfied; 71% of the diocesan priests and 58% of the religious priests said that they definitely will not leave the priesthood in the future. On the other hand, 5% of the diocesan and 14% of the religious priests said they will definitely leave, will probably leave, or are now uncertain. In this chapter we analyze the sources of satisfaction and dissatisfaction among these priests.

From the survey we know the main sources of gratification for both diocesan and religious priests. Priests feel most alive and fulfilled when they are administering the sacraments, presiding over the liturgy, preaching the Word, and helping people and families in their daily lives (Table 2.6). All research agrees on this. In contrast, priests feel the least fulfillment from administrative tasks and duties, and frustrated when overwork prevents their being pastoral leaders. These are basic facts that should orient Church leaders as they plan for the future.

To see if there are specific experiences that contribute to priestly satisfaction or dissatisfaction, we compared subgroups of priests in two ways. First, we compared those who said they will definitely not leave the priesthood with all others; second, we made a measure of satisfaction out of the items in Table 2.7 and compared priests scoring high and low on the measure. The two comparisons yielded very similar results, indicating that both measure the same thing; both serve as measures of satisfaction. Here we will look at only the first: the priests who said they will definitely not leave compared with all the others.

Do priests' backgrounds predict who will leave or not leave? We compared priests who said they definitely will not leave and other priests on
numerous background variables, including country of birth, ethnicity, undergraduate major, years of full-time employment prior to seminary, and total
years of seminary training. Only three predicted who will definitely not
leave (that is, who are satisfied). First, priests who were relatively older
when ordained were relatively more satisfied. This is consistent with the
finding in Chapter 2 that resignees were younger on average than priests
who remained in service. Second, diocesan priests were more satisfied
than religious priests. Third, priests born in the United States were more
satisfied than those born elsewhere. This third outcome is odd, because in
Chapter 2 we found that the resignees were more likely than the active
priests to have been American-born. So why do we now find in the sample
of active priests that the American-born are *more satisfied* than those born
elsewhere? We do not know; we had expected the opposite. (It is not a sta-
tistical accident, since we also found that American-born priests scored
higher on our other measure of satisfaction, not reported here.) One possibility, no more than a speculation, is that after the resignees, who were disproportionately American-born, left, the other active priests born in the
United States were *more* satisfied than average.

Other background variables had no effect on whether priests said they
will leave or stay, including West European ethnicity versus other; born
Catholic versus being a convert to Catholicism; having had a distinct spiritual awakening that led to their vocation; having gone to college seminary
versus not; having worked full-time prior to seminary versus not; having
attended a U.S. seminary versus another; and serving in the same diocese
or region in which they grew up versus not.

Specific Sources of Satisfaction or Dissatisfaction

Table 3.1 displays the priests' responses to ten specific sources of satisfaction. The "Difference" column shows that satisfaction or dissatisfaction
with the celibate life was far and away the greatest factor affecting overall
priestly satisfaction. Also important, though less so, were satisfaction with
current work in ministry, level of support received from fellow priests, and
the priest's own spiritual life. Here, then, is another piece of evidence that
problems with celibacy are the number-one vexation of newly ordained
priests today.

Table 3.2 sheds more light on satisfactions by means of assessing some
complaints voiced by the priests who were thinking of leaving. They were
more discontented than others over the living conditions in their first assignment and their present assignment, and were more discontented than others

over the lack of support from other priests. Their evaluation of the formal mentoring program was a bit more negative than the evaluation of others.

Some problems that the newly ordained face are shown in Table 3.3. The "Difference" column gives further evidence of the importance of the problems of celibacy and loneliness for newly ordained priests. Also, the problems of heavy-handed authority in the Church, of upholding some difficult Church teachings, and of always being a public person were associated with thoughts of resigning. These five seemed to be major sources of inner struggle for many of these men. On the other hand, relationships with pastors, relationships with bishops or major superiors, disagreements with other priests, inadequate salaries, and the difficulty of really reaching people today are not associated with overall priestly satisfaction or dissatisfaction. In sum, problems in priests' *personal lives* had more impact on their thoughts about staying or leaving than did problems in their *work lives*.

Table 3.1
What is Your Level of Satisfaction with the Following?
(Percent saying "Very satisfied," arranged in descending order of size of difference)

Number of cases:	Priests Who Will Never Leave (327) (%)	Priests Who May Leave (177) (%)	Difference (%)
Living a celibate life	59	12	47
Current work in ministry	74	52	22
The support you receive from fellow priests	42	20	22
Spiritual life	36	15	21
Your living situation	57	41	16
Your relationship with the bishop or superior	52	36	16
Fairness and openness in chancery decisions	29	16	13
Opportunities for continuing education	34	23	11
Your relationship with the laity with whom you work	73	64	9
Personal time schedule	24	18	6

Table 3.2
Level of Satisfaction with Specific Experiences
(In percents)

	Priests Who Will Never Leave (%)	Priests Who May Leave (%)
How would you rate your first assignment after ordination in terms of helping you make the transition from seminary to priestly ministry?		
Very helpful	48	36
Helpful	30	35
Not too helpful	17	19
Detrimental	5	10
If you were involved in a formal mentoring program after ordination [29 percent said they were], was it helpful?		
Very helpful	41	35
Helpful	43	37
Not too helpful	15	26
Detrimental	1	2
Were you satisfied or dissatisfied with your living situation in your first assignment?		
Very or somewhat satisfied	78	61
Very or somewhat dissatisfied	21	37
Don't know, or other	1	2
Are you satisfied or dissatisfied with your living situation now?		
Very or somewhat satisfied	85	76
Very or somewhat dissatisfied	13	22
Don't know, or other	2	2
Are you satisfied or dissatisfied with the help and support you receive from priests with more years of service?		
Very or somewhat satisfied	83	73
Very or somewhat dissatisfied	16	24
Don't know, or other	1	3
Are you satisfied or dissatisfied with peer support you have from other priests in your diocese or community who were ordained at about the same time?		
Very or somewhat satisfied	79	65
Very or somewhat dissatisfied	16	28
Don't know, or other	4	7

Table 3.3
Problems Which Priests Face Today
(Percent saying "A great problem," arranged from
largest to smallest difference)

	Priests Who Will Never Leave (%)	Priests Who May Leave (%)	Differ- ence (%)
Living a celibate life	3	23	20
Loneliness of priestly life	5	22	17
The way authority is too heavy-handed in the Church	4	19	15
Being expected to represent Church teachings you have difficulty with	3	18	15
Being a public person all the time	6	19	13
Difficulty of establishing private living space	7	16	9
Unrealistic demands and expectations of lay people	6	15	9
Too much work	16	23	7
Lack of agreement on what a priest is	6	11	5
Disagreement with other priests over ecclesiology and ministry	10	12	2
Your relationship with your bishop or major superior	2	4	2
Inadequate salary and benefits	5	7	2
Difficulty of really reaching people today	4	6	2
Your relationship with your pastor	7	8	1
The way authority is too lax in the Church	4	4	0

The main problems reported by happy priests—those who were certain that they will remain in the priesthood—are too much work and too much polarization among the priests over ecclesiology and ministry. Too much work is a common problem for priests, whether they are generally satisfied or not.

Younger Versus Older Priests

We said earlier that older priests were less likely to resign from the priesthood than younger ones. Were the two age groups different in other ways? To see, we split the sample of active priests into those ordained at age 34 or younger and those 35 or older.

We found that in most respects the two groups were similar. Their satisfactions and problems were similar, as were their attitudes about the Church and the priesthood. Only two small differences emerged. First, the older priests were serving in relatively smaller dioceses than the younger priests were; 76% were in dioceses with fewer than 200 priests, compared with 62% of the younger men. (Among the religious priests, we found no differences in the size of their provinces.) Second, the older priests indicated less satisfaction with peer support from other priests in their dioceses or communities who were ordained at about the same time; 30% of the older men said they were "very satisfied" with peer support, compared with 42% of the younger men. The two differences should be seen as minor. The more general picture is that the older and younger men were quite similar.

Four Examples of Satisfied Active Priests

We talked in depth with fourteen active priests in different parts of the nation. They appeared, for the most part, to be happily engaged in their ministries and free from enervating conflicts. The majority felt fulfilled and hopeful in their priesthood, even as they recounted greatly different histories and priorities.

Here we quote from four of these interviews to convey the lives of the newly ordained priests. (To preserve anonymity, we have changed the names and a few details.) The four are quite different from one another. The first, whom we call "Daniel," is a religious order priest with an active, fulfilling ministry, mostly in a high school. The second and third, "Alex" and "Bob," are diocesan priests who have diverse experiences in parish ministry. Both represent the ecclesiological attitudes of the majority of diocesan priests. The fourth, "John," typifies neoconservativism as found among a portion of the new younger priests. Taken together, the four are representative of newly ordained priests today.

Daniel: An Apostolate of Compassion

Daniel is from a Polish and Italian family in New York. His father was a naval officer who experienced long-term problems with alcohol, and this brought ongoing tension to the family life, a circumstance that Daniel mentioned over and over. Daniel and his siblings were often at church, and they knew the priests and sisters there. The priests in his parish were Dominicans, very friendly.

> They always would go out of their way to talk to you, and I remember the priests walking up and down the streets. They had their habits on and would stop and say hello. If the kids walked along, they always had candy. So my relationship with clergy was something very positive. The sisters from the school knew my mom. We knew the cook from the convent; she was a good friend of my mother's. So we were always in that kind of connection.

Daniel attended a Catholic prep school, and afterward his uncle helped him get into the police academy. When he was 18 he became a New York City policeman. It was dangerous work, and one day Daniel barely escaped being killed in a stakeout. His assistant and close partner was shot and killed in a situation in which he was ordinarily the leader and thus would have been the person to die. The episode scared Daniel and caused him to reflect on life and death. After a time he decided to look into becoming a priest. Meanwhile, alongside police work, he was taking courses at a Catholic college and received a degree.

Daniel was accepted by the Franciscans and enrolled in one of their houses of study.

> I taught high school and I lived there in the house. It's kind of, you look at them and they look at you. Most were young guys. There were about twelve of us in the house, and they had a friar and brother that were in charge of the house. And so we lived in community. Had our jobs, came back at night, prayer and evening reflection. After that year they started a new pilot program in Pennsylvania. They needed some guys who wanted to take the next step, so I agreed to go there. And I lived there and taught high school for another two years. It was a wonderful experience.

Daniel proceeded to the novitiate, and he started taking courses for a master's degree in marriage and family therapy. But he found himself in conflict with the novice director.

> The novice director was this guy who was very much into psychobabble, one of these psychologist types, and he started analyzing people. I already had my degree in psychology, and I would always challenge him. He didn't like that. He was not impressed with that. He gave me a hard time, but I had a spiritual director that was also on the team who was very supportive, and one time I had found out some information about the director through a friend, that he had taken a couple of the novices on vacation. They had this big wild party, and so on and so on, and I had gotten this information. He was greatly upset that I knew about this and kind of interrogated me, and he said, "I'm going to make your life hell."

Subsequently Daniel found out that the novice director had recommended that he not be allowed to continue in the community, and he could do nothing to overturn it. He had to leave. In anger and frustration, he withdrew from the community. A year later, after cooling off, he turned to the Oblates and was accepted by them for the novitiate. It went well, and Daniel began studying theology at a university-related seminary in the East. He finished theology and a earned a master's degree in psychology. One day his boss called him to ask if he could come to an all-boys,' African-American high school run by the Oblates. After much hesitation Daniel said yes, and now he has taught there happily for ten years.

After six years at the high school, Daniel pursued ordination. He took several refresher courses in liturgy and reconciliation, did his internship as a deacon, and was ordained. He was then 40 years old. Soon he began working toward a doctorate of ministry at a Catholic seminary and in time earned the degree. Today he continues as a priest and teacher at the high school, is an associate in two parishes, and leads missions and retreats. He feels blessed.

> I love what I do, and I love presiding at Eucharist. I love the sacramental life that's present to people in those moments of union. Being with couples preparing for marriage, celebrating their love. Even being with people to share their pain and their sorrow. And it's been so powerful for me and so painful at times, because I can't see how a priest can just get up there and just go through the motions. I can't get through weddings and funerals without being in tears half the time. I've got to be real. I've got to be who I am, and if that's shedding a tear or hugging someone and crying with them, for me that's real. Going to hospitals is one of the hardest things for me, because my family is so health-conscious. Whenever I have to go, beforehand I always go to the nursery so I can see new life and the whole gift of life, and I leave with that.

> I love working with young people. A lot of my experience growing up, knowing what I went through, and the pain at home, because my mom was so absorbed with my father and keeping the family together. Physical things got neglected. Our teeth got neglected. I had acne really bad as a kid, and that was never taken care of. And so I went through a lot of that embarrassment as a teenager and was called all kinds of names, and never wanted to date or do anything like that, because I just felt no one would like me. I wasn't attractive—while my brothers were big athletes, very attractive. So I really had to work on my self-image. People liked me because I was a jokester, with a great sense of humor.

Daniel finds that being in a religious community is important. He could never be a diocesan priest, since diocesan priesthood doesn't include the community life that he finds so precious.

For me, the only way priesthood works in my own life is if I have the support of brothers, certainly of the community of the Church, certainly of other guys that are in this together. I need that support, and I found that in our community. The Midwest church and the province where I am, was just a phenomenal group of men. They were real. They had a support group for priests dealing with alcoholism and for the few guys that had any past or anything having to do with drugs. They had gay support groups for men dealing with their sexual orientation and how that is to be integrated into who they are. They had a Hispanic support group. So that whole mix of who this community and province was, it was just so attractive to me. I wanted to be a part of something like that.

Interviewer: "It sounds as if your community life has been very life-giving."

Yeah. And it's a two-edged sword. You get guys that drive you crazy. It's like a family. When you look at your brothers and sisters, some of them you get along with more than others. Others drive you up a wall, but that's real. You can't pick who your brothers and sisters are going to be in life. And I can't pick who I'm going to live with. You've got to make it work. So what we do, I feel, is to model Christian living for the world. To show that it is possible for all of us to get along and work together even if we are African-American, Hispanic, Asian, gay, straight, old, young, we can still make it happen. That's what it is for me.

Community living has been good. The guys are good. You certainly find one or two guys that you could really tell it all to. The guys are going to give you a kick in the ass when you need it and say, "What are you doing? What's going on here?" And we need that. When we can build on that kind of trust, and we can really challenge one another and not play games, and live honestly. That's what it's about. I've been blessed in this province to always have been in communities where we can, for the most part, be honest. And if people are not, we challenge them.

The interviewer asked if Daniel was faced with unrealistic expectations from the laity.

Yeah. I'm a formal associate in two parishes, and I'm involved in all the parochial stuff, education, wedding prep, baptisms, the whole sacramental thing. I really love it. I really enjoy it. But I don't have enough time in the day to do everything. Thank God I have the energy for it. Maybe the day will come when my energy will slow down. I'm sure it will, but for now I can do this. I can be full-time at the high school, I can also teach at the seminary. I do adult education at two or three parishes. I do parish missions. This is the third year in which I had five parish missions in a row. Five weekends in a row. And the money I raise goes to support some boys at the high school. I have to balance that with my community life. I could be gone every night. I could go from school, get in my car, and drive to a parish to a night of recollection and confirmation talk. And the list goes on and on. I do dozens a year. So I have to really balance that. Some of the guys will say, "We haven't seen you all week. You've been checked out all week for supper." If community life is important to me, I have got to put my money where my mouth is.

Interviewer: "Where will you be in the next five years? What's down the line?"

I have always loved and would love to get into retreat ministry. I got my license in massage therapy and spirituality at _____, did a whole program on that. What I would like to do is really put together a program where I can incorporate spiritual direction, preaching, group retreats, my message, and all that into a holistic spirituality center. One of my classmates started a center in Arizona. It's on the top of a mountain, and it just sounds so attractive. So that's really my dream and my hope. I would love to get into that kind of ministry.

I would have to live in community. In our order we can't live outside of three or four guys. But we could choose our own ministry if we had three or four guys who wanted to get into this ministry, or any kind of ministry. The community is our life together. It's like a family. You go out and work and you come back home to the family. You've got to make time just like anyone else for your family. We're all busy. We all have meetings and extra things that we do. How do we balance all that? Plus our prayer life.

Interviewer: "As you look back at your formation, what do you think were some of the critical things?"

I had mentors, priests, in my life who were very honest, who were real for me. They were good role models. They were challenging. They got me to ask the right questions. They didn't pull any punches. They said this is tough work, and you're going to be exhausted. You have a lot to do, but it's like the Marine Corps. It's the hardest job you'll ever have.

Daniel saw his ministry to students as the main thing.

If I'm on the phone, I have three letters in front of me, and I'm typing something on the computer, and a kid comes and knocks on the door, I want to be able to stop everything I'm doing and show him that he is the most important thing to me. That's what meant something to me when I was young. Am I always one hundred percent successful in that? No. Do sometimes I growl and the kid will say, "You're in a bad mood; I'll come back when you're in a better mood." Yes. But then I feel guilty and I seek them out and say I'm really sorry. I'm just having a bad day.

He summed up his satisfactions:

I want to be with people who are out there and who encourage and empower the lay people. I don't want men who are threatened by lay leadership. I love our diocese because we have men and women, married couples, and people that are actively involved in positions in the parish in all kinds of ways. I get frightened when I hear stuff that comes down from Rome trying to limit that. You hear the old boys' club saying to keep the lay people in their place. It's a power trip. It's the boys' club. I'm not threatened by empowering laity. I welcome the help. I think they need to be trained just like we need to be trained.

Daniel reflected on the shortage of vocations in his community.

I think that we need to discern the ability to relate in priests. What happens when we get hard up for bodies is we'll take whatever and anything. That happens in a lot of communities. But we really have to do a discernment process. . . . We really have some jerks. There are lots of guys that have done enough damage. My mom was yelled at by a priest. When she was 29, she had five of us. And she and my father decided to practice birth control. She went into the confessional and the priest yelled and screamed at her, told her she was going to hell, that if she didn't stop practicing birth control, not to set foot in the church again. My mother never went back to church until my ordination, to receive communion. She would go to a wedding or funeral certainly, but not to be at a Mass or participate in any way, because of this guy.

Everything I have read in my study of the Gospel is that Jesus wants men and women of heart. Not of rules. Rules are hard as rock, and we don't need that. The Church will survive. The Holy Spirit has kept the Church for many years. It doesn't need the liturgy police out there making sure people are kneeling at the right time. I got involved in AIDS hospice work, and you deal with a lot of the gay community. And just to listen to their pain. These are good Catholic people who have been shunned by the Church and hurt by the Church. You want to walk with them. You want to minister to them and you see what the system has done to people and has hurt people like my mom. And the divorced and remarried. All those issues that we find real difficult and that the official position kind of condemns. How do we minister pastorally in the image of Jesus?

It's a struggle, because I have to represent the official position of the Church as a priest. I have to be the voice of the Church in the world, but for me, I have to be the compassion of Jesus in the world. And for me that's more important than being the voice of the Church. So that's how I've survived and that's certainly how I feel supported by my community. I have to be Jesus' eyes and his hands for the world.

I love my Church. And I always say, for me the Church is the people. We have a system, a hierarchy. But it's bigger than that. It's more than that. So the way I survive is by looking at a wider, more expansive notion of Church. It's not just loyalty. We are the Body of Christ. We are the Church and the main thing is loyalty to that, and preaching the Gospel. Jesus constantly throughout the Gospel came up against the church of his day and called them to task, called them back to the compassion of God. That's what I try to do.

Our work has to be prayerful, and prayer has to be part of our lives. We need the mark of Mary. You've got to take time; otherwise we're running around doing great work, but it's not connected. Prayer has to be important in formation, so that you fall in love with the Lord and with God, which is what it's all about.

Alex: Coping Well Under the Pressure

Alex is an only child of immigrants from Eastern Europe now living in an Eastern state. His mother liked the idea of having a son who was a priest, and his aunt was a Dominican nun. This seemed to have had an effect on him. He took religious education seriously even at a young age. For years he was an altar server, and his family took him to numerous diocesan events such as installations of bishops. He attended Catholic high school and thought often about the priesthood.

After high school he entered college seminary. Because the seminary was associated with a university, he met girls there. His junior year in seminary was one of ambivalence.

It was leading me to some real questioning of celibacy. And I was looking at my family life and thinking "I'd really like to have a wife and children." So junior year became a very big year of questioning and really looking at what I was doing. About halfway through I was really thinking about leaving the seminary and doing something else. My dad was a teacher, and I thought maybe I'd want to be a teacher. So I started thinking about that, and really the question of celibacy was starting to hit home. I called it my "dark days."

In my senior year we had about fifteen in my class, and it was coming to the time for applying to a seminary for theology. A lot of the guys were deciding not to go on. We ended up having three of us go on out of that class of fifteen. About ten decided not to go on, and I think celibacy was the big thing for them. My best friends were not going on, and that was starting to have an effect on me. But I went to the interview for entering theology, and it was with a lay couple. It was an incredible interview. I came out really charged up and saying the priesthood is for me.

That same day my best friend decided that he wasn't going on. It was due to celibacy for him. He wanted to have a wife, wanted to have a family. This was on the same day. But through this whole thing at college, I was looking at celibacy through a negative view, what I wasn't going to have, as opposed to what celibacy could be. I want to make that distinction here because it's a big one, and there was a shift in my way of looking at it when I went on to seminary for theology. The difference was that at the major seminary it was a positive focus, stressing the relationship one has with God through celibacy as opposed to what one wasn't going to have because one was celibate. I looked at the relationship that one could have with God and with people in the parish as positively living out what celibacy meant.

Senior year at the college seminary came to a crashing halt for me. I called my parents to the seminary one day and I basically told them I wasn't going on. Mom and Dad were both kind of devastated at that point, because they were pretty grounded in the fact that this was what I was going to do with my life. But they supported me in what I wanted to do.

So I'd basically decided that I wasn't going to go on to seminary. This was in April. About that time I was coming back one afternoon from visiting my mom and dad, and a friend of mine was in the parking lot talking to some young ladies. He called me over and introduced me, and I really clicked with the one young lady. And I thought, "Hmm, well, God answered my prayers when I was asking, 'What do you want me to do?' Isn't this something? Out in the middle of the parking lot I meet somebody and we click! Maybe this is His answer." The next day I got her phone number and we struck up a friendship. And after graduation in the summer I'm still becoming better friends with this young woman. But the decision that I thought was going to bring me peace, deciding not to become a priest, it was eating away at me like crazy. What I thought was going to bring me peace [leaving the seminary] put me in more turmoil than I'd ever been in before. I really, really hit prayer hard and was talking with my spiritual director. I applied to major seminary and was accepted. I was really kind of in a mess at that point, as far as knowing what to do. Should I go on? The spiritual director is saying, "Well, why don't you try it for a year? See what it's like." And I said okay. And the young woman and I became friends. We weren't really dating, just friends. And as soon as I shifted back to going to seminary, my peace returned.

After I began seminary this friendship [with the girl] was going on, and we'd meet for lunch periodically. I was very careful with it, though. I don't know whether it was good or bad, but there was this sense at the seminary that you have to watch your friendships. That was the idea they communicated. You don't want to get too close, you've got to be careful of that. If you're living the celibate life, you've got to watch those kinds of things so you don't convey the wrong message and show that you're not living a double kind of life. If you're going to live celibacy, you've got to live it. And this is a fine-line struggle, even to this day I think of how you can have relationships that are true friendships without conveying the wrong thing to people. I think it's healthy to have friendships with women, appropriately. But I think there is also a sense on some people's parts that it is too much of a challenge to one's celibacy.

And I had another really good friend too. She was about ten years older than me, but we were really good friends. We'd go out to movies and stuff, out to dinner. But those relationships didn't take me away from that call. They helped, especially when I went into the major seminary, they really helped. I made it clear that this is a friendship, that's what it is. I'm not in this for a dating relationship, and I'm very happy with what I'm doing and where I'm going. But even among the guys at the seminary there was a sense that this isn't a healthy kind of thing for celibacy and for a person who is becoming a priest.

I think there were times when friendships with women were looked down upon by administration or by faculty. If they were getting too close, there was kind of a pulling aside of either the student or the other person he was friends with, and they'd say, "We think this is a little too close."

Is Alex in favor of having women in the same classes with seminarians?

I really think that is important, because 80 percent of parish work involves women in one way or another. And this is why I think it's a danger for some of the guys who were looking at relationships with women as being something to stay away from, because then you're not going to be able to deal well with it in the parish. If you're pushing that away now, you're going to be in big trouble later relating on the parish level.

Alex liked the intellectual part of seminary.

A great thing about the seminary is that they put you in touch with all kinds of different theologies across the board. Some people took offense at that—that they were putting us in touch with some of the more cutting-edge things at times. People thought the classes were teaching that as opposed to teaching authentic, orthodox Catholicism or something like that.

There was a big shift going on when I was in the seminary from '92 to '97. By the end there were more guys coming in from a conservative perspective. Some guys were really wanting to get back to cassocks and some kind of nostalgic stuff. To use the theological terms, a high Christology and just a different look at priesthood and what it was about and what it meant.

Alex enjoyed his time at both the college seminary and the theologate. He contrasted himself with a number of other seminarians who thought seminary life was too controlling.

They looked at some of the things the seminary did as being authoritarian or controlling. Especially when it came to some guys being asked not to continue. That was always a big sticking point with a lot of guys. I had a very different perspective than a lot of guys on that. I put faith that these people on the faculty were chosen by the bishop to help in formation, and they have more knowledge than I'll ever have of the situation. That put me at odds with a lot of the other students.

Alex praised his field education during the semesters and in the summer. One fieldwork experience was in hospitals, and it forced him to overcome his fear of hospitals. Now he is able to visit people in the hospital without anxiety. Best of all was the year-long internship after second-year theology.

The internship brought me into contact with people where they were, regular parish people, not really concerned about some of these things that were major theological discussions.

Alex was ordained at age 27. He had gone straight through without stopping. At the time of the interview, he had been in the priesthood three years in one assignment. He talked about his parish.

I definitely felt prepared, as much as I could be. There are some things that there is absolutely no way you could be prepared for. There is so much just day-to-day living. For one thing, in seminary you weren't responsible for saying Masses, which is a big part of what you do later. Going from daily liturgy to a funeral, to a wedding, to the anticipated Mass for Sunday. The whole presiding and the whole connectedness to families in grief, to families in joy, to an anticipated Mass for the weekend—incredibly challenging. And keeping all of that straight. One of the images that came up in the seminary is, you're kind of like the leader of a jazz band.

Alex told of his priest mentor. He was asked to pick one from a list, and he picked a priest he knew. The mentoring had been wonderful. The official mentorship program was to last only one year, but Alex wanted to continue, and they still meet. His relationships with other priests have been less important.

It's tough, because in my class there were three of us that were ordained. Two of us were together in college seminary and in theology. We talk but we're both very busy, and it's hard to get together. We're living too far apart. I try to make sure that I'm at priest functions and priest funerals, the convocations, the picnics, whatever is there for bringing us together. It's very supportive. A lot of this is what you make of it.

What, in Alex's experience, has been the most encouraging part of being a priest?

The biggest thing is people. People are so supportive. I mean, you get your occasional anonymous critical letter that you should probably just throw away. But people are so supportive. Coming into this parish, guys were saying to me, "People aren't friendly there." But coming in, I let the experience be for itself. I learned that a long time ago. It was a good lesson in life, to go into things and let it be for itself, as opposed to going with those major expectations of something. I found the people here just wonderfully welcoming and completely opposite of what all kinds of people were saying.

Has anything been discouraging?

Sometimes you like a little more feedback on something. From staff members or parishioners, across the board. Sometimes you want to know, did that touch somebody? Did this go well? And it's not like I'm looking for a reward for something, but the feedback is delayed. It's just "Nice job" or something like that, but could you tell me more about that?

Another thing. Sometimes you get times where, especially in dealing with people who are sick and the bereaved, you get a whole bunch of that piled up. Then it seems like every person who is sick is coming down with something so fatal that there is no hope for getting better, barring any miracles. You kind of take several body blows all at once, and it can be tough. Communion calls are so wonderful, but they are also very tough. Emotionally it's draining. To drive by all the places as you're going on Communion calls where you used to stop and bring Communion, and now all these people are dead.

Sometimes the hours are long. One week I decided I'm going to add up my hours just to know where the time goes. I think I got to Thursday, and it was already at sixty-nine hours or something like that. So I didn't even get to the weekend, as far as weekend stuff. I was just like, "I'm not counting anymore. I don't want to see this." It makes it difficult to balance everything, to balance prayer, to balance exercise, to balance all those things that you really need to have a balanced life.

I think you have to be careful of expectations. As much as possible you try to be there, but you've got to know when to say, "No, I can't do this. Let's look for a different way of going about this. Can someone other than the priest celebrate a prayer service for this occasion?" This is one of the best things to come out of the fact that there are fewer priests: that laity is taking on its role as part of the community and doing leadership and all of that. That is so important. How do we delegate, how do we encourage people to take on that role in the fullness that it's meant to be? Collaboration is so necessary to parishes today.

Bishop _____ just came out with a letter about keeping things in perspective. I found that very good. Letting guys know that it's okay to say no to things. I think a lot of guys still come out with the messiah complex, to be all things to all people, always and everywhere. But that's not healthy. You've got to take time for yourself, you've got to take time for retreat. That is something I struggled with early on, trying to balance getting in vacation, retreat time, and continuing things. There is only so much time you can be away, between yourself and the pastor.

And prayer. Prayer is so important too. If you want to talk about something that's been difficult and sometimes discouraging for myself, the toughest thing is that Liturgy of Hours. Doing that every day, trying to pray it instead of just saying it. Fitting that prayer in as well as other kinds of prayer, prayer that one finds important to one's own personal spirituality, it's juggling and really tough sometimes. Liturgy of Hours helps me really ground myself. I need to do this; this one's required. Which one wins? It's something I work through with my spiritual director. Every priest should have one. I don't know that I would survive without one.

> Feelings of loneliness I see as a call from God, as if God were saying to me, "Come and talk to me. You have been away from me too long." It is a call from God to prayer, not an emptiness that needs to be filled by diversions, movies, or running away.

Alex maintained his friendship with the woman he went out with while in college seminary. Later he served as a witness at her wedding. For years they have been a mutual support for each other, and she is now pursuing studies for lay pastoral ministry in another diocese.

Bob: Successful in Overcoming Difficulties

Bob was ordained at 35, and he was 40 when we talked with him. He was the youngest of eight children of Irish immigrants. His family life was tumultuous, partly because his father was an alcoholic. In addition to that, his brothers and sisters dabbled in the hippy movement. Bob was the youngest and grew up in reaction to these excesses of his siblings. When he was in high school, his parents split up.

Bob had had little interest in Catholicism as a youth. He went away to college, earned a bachelor's degree in business, and soon went to work in a stockbroking firm. Two years later, he entered graduate school at a state university and earned an MBA. During his graduate study, a friend invited him to a musical program at the campus ministry, and he went.

> Well, the parish on the university campus is a very vibrant parish, and when I went there I was shocked, because the church probably had seating for about a thousand people, and it was full. It was vibrant, not charismatic, but quite a vibrant liturgy and it was mostly young adults—students and professors. And it just didn't make sense at all, because my formula was you go to church so long as your parents make you, and these people obviously are away at college. What the heck are they doing at church? And there was an energy there. There was a reason why people were there.

Bob was curious and later went back. The preaching was excellent. It caused him to be more open to experiences of the Spirit.

After the MBA, Bob moved to the Northeast and became a partner in a new research firm. The firm did well, and soon Bob bought his own house. He did lots of reading, including the works of Thomas Merton.

> I can't tell you the day, but at one point I remember saying to myself, "The world makes more sense from a Christian perspective. In the light of faith, the world makes more sense to me." I guess I affirmed my belief and my Catholicity. I had looked at other churches as well and had visited them. What kept me in the Catholic Church, although I didn't buy into everything at that point, was a strong sense of lineage, the fact that the Catholic Church

didn't spin off from something else. So I stuck with the Catholic Church and the universal nature of it, those two things.

Bob was now 30.

> One day I just thought to myself, "You're meant to be a priest." I remember the minute. It became an obsessive thought. I had always intended to get married and have a family, yet the priesthood was a thought that was always there in the back of my mind. I had had serious relationships, not at that time specifically, but I had dated women for some long periods. In high school I dated one girl for three years. In college and after that I dated one girl for five years, and I had intended to find the right one and get married. So the implications of the thought that priesthood was calling were radical. After a month of almost obsessing over it, I called the vocation director in the diocese and started a series of interviews and meetings with a group of men considering priesthood.

A few months later Bob entered theological seminary. He sold his house. His family and friends were partly supportive, partly inquisitive.

> My mother and sister, the people closest to me, all were very supportive. Other siblings maybe questioned my motives. "Why is he doing this? Is he running away from something? Is he giving up on women?" And my friends as well. "How can you give up what you've achieved?" So from my immediate family I had support. From others, support but also questioning. They didn't take it at face value.

> The first year of seminary was difficult. I went from a five-bedroom house to a cell. And also I felt like I was back on the bottom rung of the totem pole again. I had worked very hard and had sacrificed a lot. Getting to where I'd gotten meant a lot of sacrifices, and I was proud of where I had gotten, based on the fact that I wasn't coming from a wealthy family who supported me through. I kind of fought my way up. Now here I am, I'm on the same level with these guys who are just coming out of undergraduate school. So it was a mixture of guys right out of undergraduate and guys who were like myself, second career. That was a bit of a rude awakening. So I remember there being a lot of mixed emotions. I was overjoyed about being there. I was in awe of the fact that I was there, because it was even surprising to me. There was some level of, I don't want to use the word "depression," but melancholy at times, because here I am in this one room. I felt like I was being treated like a kid sometimes. We delayed vocations were a fairly new phenomenon, and I don't think the faculty were really very familiar with dealing with guys on very different levels of maturation. And they talked to all of us the same.

> Academically it was difficult. I had already been through a tough graduate school program with a double major. So that was rigorous, but this was different. Both of my degrees were very technically oriented, and so when I

started with the philosophy and theology, it was a whole new way of thinking that I was not accustomed to. It was academically a bit belittling to me.

Interviewer: "How about the formation program?"

The formation director that I had was somebody who had been a pastor for a number of years and had come back and was doing formation work, so he was very much in touch with the dynamics of parish life. It was very good working with him. He was helpful. The spiritual director that I chose was very much like the priest in my home parish years ago, an old, quiet, unassuming, very saintly man. That worked well, having the both of them. I felt free to be very open with them. Other guys would complain about the risk in being extremely reticent or being totally open, because they felt that these things would be used against them. I never felt that way. Also the apostolic work was good. First I was working in some organization dealing directly with the poor, which I think was very good. Difficult for me, again, because I'd never done it before. Scared. I don't know how to talk to very poor people, especially poor people who are mentally handicapped. I worked with a mental health organization. So it was a difficult experience, but I learned a lot and grew a lot as a result.

My second year was in a modified CPE program, clinical pastoral training. It was earth-shattering but in a way good, because I did not know how to handle a lot of the emotions that I was experiencing, or didn't know how to articulate them. I've done a lot of reading, and I think this is very common to adult children of alcoholics. They can't express emotion and so forth. So I was thrown into this shark-infested pool of emotions. The experience was hard, again, but very good. It was salvific in the sense that the magic of CPE awakened in me an ability to express emotion, feel emotion, deal with it on a healthy level. Some guys were threatened by it, and some were leaving the seminary as a result. I was afraid of it too, but I also saw that it was going to save me in a sense.

Did Bob have good friends in seminary?

I quickly learned that there's something about this incubator experience that's a very unnatural mode of living. And that mode of living produces a lot of feelings, actions, emotions in guys that would otherwise seem a bit weird. I quickly kind of became the ringleader of my classmates from our diocese. There were about five or six of us, and I would plan opportunities for us to get together regularly. Tried having one night a week when we'd all eat together. Occasionally get together to pray together and things like that. That's just my organizational nature, so it came out in that way, and I made two good friends in the seminary. I also had well-formed relationships outside the seminary and so probably I didn't have any real soul mate in the seminary. Good friends and acquaintances, but my soul mates were outside the seminary, from the body of friends I had before going in.

Bob was ordained when he was 35.

> I felt very prepared at the end of seminary. I felt very confident that I could function. That was probably naive confidence.

He was assigned to a suburban parish.

> I felt very welcomed there and very energized, and the pastor with whom I was assigned was a great guy. But without a shadow of a doubt he was clinically depressed. He was extremely cynical. He would go through the motions on a very minimalistic level, which had its good and bad side for me. It was very difficult living with him.
>
> Inside the rectory I did not feel supported at all. I had quickly gotten my feet wet and started doing pastoral work. The pastor wouldn't even ask me how it went. Nothing like "Did anybody show up?" or whatever. So I wasn't feeling very supported. And living in the rectory as well, just having meals together and whatnot, that was very difficult. Because if he was in a good mood, great. But if he was in a bad mood, how do you sit through dinner and not say a word? Very tense, very painful.
>
> Outside the rectory I felt very affirmed. The plus side for me was that the pastor said to me shortly after I was there, he said, "It's all yours. Do whatever you want. You want to be pastor? Here, you do it." So I took the ball and ran with it. There wasn't a social concerns ministry, so I got something there. There was no youth group. We got something going there. There was no RCIA [Rite of Christian Initiation of Adults] program. We got something there. I thrive on the organizational level, getting people excited about things and the people saw something new happening and really did lend me a lot of support, and they trusted me. So we got a lot of good things going, adult education and things like that.
>
> I made a decision after three years that I wanted to change parishes. The life inside the rectory I felt was damaging to my own mental health. I had tried to do something about it. I had spoken to the pastor, but he was not willing to listen. He was self-destructive, going on eating binges of doughnuts or cake. This was his solace. There'd be days where I wouldn't see him. He'd never come out of his room. He might go say the daily Mass, but then quickly retreat to his room. I was really concerned about his well-being.

Later Bob felt he had to speak to the regional bishop about the pastor. They agreed that Bob needed to move to another parish.

> During this time I was doing other things. I love to do interesting travel, so one year I went to Costa Rica and trekked around. Hiked in Scotland another year. So travel was the main thing. Jogging. I jogged regularly, so I had that as an outlet. And social too. As I said, I have a few good friends, and I get to-

gether with them as frequently as possible. And I was also invited out a lot to parishioners' homes. I enjoyed that.

After three years Bob was moved to a very large suburban parish that had three priests and lots of action. Bob became overbusy.

> The rectory life is fine here. I get along very well the pastor and the other associate. They are both energetic and dedicated to the ministry. So rectory life is good, although we're all so busy we rarely all eat together.

Bob is looking ahead. He is now working on a doctor of ministry degree, and as part of that he's doing a project he likes. His heart is in it. He wants to develop models for human resource management on a parish level and to give training seminars on it.

> From my observation I think most pastors do a pretty good job, but they rely on the nice-guy approach. Pastors are basically nice guys. They want what is best for their employees and staff members and volunteers, for the most part. But I've also found that most of them do not have the basic skills to do it in a more efficient way. It's not to turn them into junior executives but basically to say, "Here are proven methods to achieve a level of teamwork and motivation among staff members." My heart's in that, and I see a real need for it. There are many pastors who feel a level of frustration, and sometimes they feel incompetent and even articulate it.

Interviewer: "What do you see in your future?"

> In terms of the future, I'm not exactly sure how that will unravel, but I would like to pursue that human resource idea in some way, maybe provide it as maybe a service to the diocese. And I do look forward to being a pastor. I feel much more energetic when I have the wherewithal, the chance, to be creative and get people excited and try to rally them around a common cause. I'm just not in a position to do that now, so I look forward to that as well.

John: Inspired by Pope John Paul II

John was one of six children in a middle-class Midwestern suburban family. He attended Catholic school but didn't think about the priesthood until he was 21. At the time he was in college, studying accounting.

> I always had a mildly philosophical bent, just pondering life, and I thought it might be a good idea to find out more about the religion you claim to have, so I went and bought a Bible. I remember it well: "The Words of Jesus in Red Ink." Probably it wasn't a Catholic Bible, but I just began to read that and to meditate on that. And that's where it began.

John thought about the priesthood and decided to contact the diocesan vocation director. After much reading and praying he gave seminary a try.

Interviewer: "Did you have a period of time in your young adult years when you dated? Did you think about the whole piece of celibacy?"

> I had a girlfriend at the end of eighth grade for about two years. And in high school I had another girlfriend. We dated about two years. Beyond that, in college, there were people I dated for a while, but nothing of that duration. In my discernment I always felt like that was the only thing I was discerning: whether to be married or to be a priest. I've always been somewhat of an independent soul. So I didn't feel it would be unreasonable for me to be celibate.

He began theology at the diocesan seminary. It was a huge disappointment.

> At any given point in my first year and a half in seminary, I could have left on a dime. And in fact at one point I had made up my mind to go. I had a job lined up, and I was just waiting until the end of the semester to do it.

Interviewer: "Why?"

> Because I just found the seminary to be an abysmal place. It was simply the contrary of everything I was setting out to do in my life. I should mention that right before beginning seminary I went to World Youth Day in Denver, a ten-day bus trip with college students. Plus the impact the Holy Father made on me. If I hadn't had those ten days, I can guarantee I wouldn't have lasted the first year. It was simply ten days of perpetual prayer and catechism. And that's really when my roots began to grow. And then I went to seminary in a place that was really opposed to Catholicism. It was just the polar opposite of everything I was seeking to do.

Interviewer: "How did you reconcile that? How did you work through it?"

> Well, the first thing is that I was there to help my own soul to be formed, so I did that. I had time to get together a prayer life, and I got some good roots going in that. The student body was simply outstanding. The class that began with me were just wonderful young men. We all felt the same way, and there was a great camaraderie amongst us. And it helped me to realize that I'm not from another planet. I started with twenty guys, and eighteen felt the same way. So that was good. And then I did keep working at the store on weekends and a couple nights a week, unbeknownst to the seminary faculty. That was a wonderful out for me. It was ten hours a week in a normal environment, and that was nice.

John felt like switching to another seminary, and two of his buddies did ask the bishop to let them transfer. But John was cautious about asking the bishop for a change, so he continued in spite of his dislike of the place.

Academically, the faculty certainly knew I wasn't of their mindset, if you will. Every class that I had would invariably end up being a course in dissent. But when I wrote my paper at the end, I would go through the Pope and Balthasar and Ratzinger and simply write the opposite of what I had been taught. That way I was learning what the Church taught, and I could feel with some integrity that the faculty knew I wasn't buying in. I wasn't pretending I did. And I just left it on the table and things just went along that way.

Interviewer: "It sounds as if you didn't have much support from the faculty."

Well, you see, our class was sort of a shock to them because we were the first orthodox class. We loved the Pope, we prayed our rosaries, we couldn't wait for the new catechism to come out. The Universal Catechism. We wanted John Paul canonized while he is still alive. They had had an occasional orthodox guy, but that was the first time it happened in such numbers.

John was restless and thought about leaving the diocese. He went to live with a religious order for a while but then realized that it wasn't a good fit, so he returned to the seminary.

Interviewer: "In your seminary, was the course content also a source of disillusionment, or just the people?"

No, the course quality was very poor for the most part. There was usually one solid course I could focus on that would make it bearable. My Church history classes were very good. My canon law teacher was excellent. . . . There were a couple of really outstanding faculty members.

Interviewer: "What kept you going for four years? What was it that urged you on?"

Well, a lot of it was resolved halfway through my second year. I went to Rome and met the Pope, and that was a turning point. I simply knew I was called to be a priest.

Interviewer: "Explain to me about meeting the Pope. Was it actually meeting him?"

Being in Rome was a big part of me, praying at the shrines. But simply meeting the Pope, who I think is just the perfect embodiment of the priesthood. And I felt in my heart how profound the priesthood is when lived well. Just being in his presence was the end to the doubts as to whether or not I was called to the priesthood.

There were other pieces as well. There was my own prayer life, which was nothing I had preplanned. It took me a year to pray through *The Imitation of Christ,* and that was the first book I read in seminary. I spent hour upon hour in front of the Blessed Sacrament, praying that and having it sink into me. I couldn't quote you a single verse out of that, but it becomes a part of who you are. *The Dialogue of Saint Catherine* would be the same thing. I spent a couple of years reading that, and all these things went into forming my soul.

Interviewer: "Were you receiving spiritual direction at the seminary?"

Yeah, we always had a spiritual director. That was okay, just okay. It was average. He was a good man, had my best interests at heart, but there wasn't a real strong connection, which was more my fault. I wasn't a good directee. I never really understood what it was supposed to be about. We had very different spiritual values, but we were able to respect one another.

Interviewer: "Did you have close friends at the seminary? Guys you could talk to on more than just a superficial level?"

Oh sure. They're still my friends for that reason.

Interviewer: "Did you have field education during seminary?"

Yeah, during second theology. It was in a retirement community.

Interviewer: "How was that?"

Silly, for the most part. We weren't allowed to wear clericals. We were just supposed to be people's buddies, knock on their doors, shoot the breeze, and talk about their medication. The woman who was our supervisor requested that we not wear our clericals. It seemed quite silly to me. I was training to be a priest, and when I go to visit people, it is as a priest, with the Eucharist, with the Bible. That's what we do. So why would I be training to do something different? It seemed a little inane. But it was fun. The woman had a great personality, had great commonsense advice, and it was useful in that regard.

And after second theology I had the pastoral year in a parish. That was wonderful. That was when I could finally see if I could be a priest. Would I be any good at it? I had to give homilies, even though I shouldn't have. That was the context in which I saw people. I visited people who were shut-ins, in the hospital, went to the classrooms, taught religious education. I was doing the closest things to priestly work a nonpriest can do. And it was reassuring to see that I felt like I was doing what I was supposed to do. By doing those things, I never felt more myself. Not what I was supposed to do when someone gave me orders, but in that this was really what I was meant to do. It was more than an intellectual agreement. In day-to-day life it really felt like what God meant for me to do. People were very gracious and responded well.

The third and fourth years of seminary were a bit different. Once a seminarian comes back from his pastoral year and is sent back to seminary, that is understood as the bishop saying he intends to ordain the man. So the faculty, in a sense, gives up on you. [Laugh.] You're allowed to live a little more freely and remember that you're a grown-up. So the last two years were a little bit better. Not like the first two years, which was a childish existence.

John explained that his seminary class was different from any prior class.

I think it was a very warped environment. I think the faculty as a whole felt threatened by the orthodox incoming class. And I was maybe one of the more vocal ones. In our first year there were four classes ahead of us at the seminary, and while it was for the most part a very friendly existence, the older students would say, "They don't know what to do with you guys." And every class after us was the same. Orthodox. I think it was just fifteen years of Pope John Paul paying off more than anything. It's amazing how many incoming seminarians list specifically his papacy in some way as what brought them to think about the priesthood.

John was ordained a priest at age 29, and when we talked he had served a year and a half in his first assignment.

Interviewer: "Do you have a good mentor?"

There is a mentor program, and the priest who is my mentor is a fantastic priest. I think that the program is well intended but unnecessary. At this point you're a grown man, you have friends, and there are people who you will talk to and get advice from. If you're someone who doesn't want to talk to someone to get advice, forcing him to have a mentor [is useless]. They're just going to kill the hour with prattle anyway. So I understand what led to the program being put into place, I just don't think it accomplishes that on a day-to-day level. For me there wasn't a whole lot to talk about, so I didn't want to give him another meeting.

The interviewer asked John if he thought he could fit into the Church today. Many people see the Church as needing to be more open, with incorporation of women, married clergy, and those sorts of issues.

I think that is very much a generational thing. I'm certainly not a product of the 1970s, so I don't share that same worldview. I want to be faithful to the Catholic Church as it exists, not as I seek to remake it. Here in this diocese I think simply being faithful to the Church puts you in a minority. For me, day-to-day, I just have to live as well as I can and as faithfully as I can.

Interviewer: "Do you see the Church in this diocese as different from how you yourself see the Church and its mission?"

Everyone in our diocese is very nice to one another. But I think we essentially belong to different religions in a lot of ways. I think in the Bible, John and Peter had differences of personality, and that's fine. I think John and Judas, that's a very different contrast. So if I like to use gold chalices and baroque vestments and another priest likes a clay chalice and a poncho, well, okay. But I don't see that as being interchangeable with being faithful to the Church teachings and deciding which ones you're going to change. It's not a question if there are differences. Of course there are differences. Are the differences differences in essence? I think, yes, they are.

Interviewer: "If you did not feel encouragement as a priest, if people did not like you as a priest here, how would you deal with that?"

Well, I think it would depend on what they weren't liking or what I was not liking. If they did not like the fact that they had a priest against birth control and abortion, they can go on not liking me all they want. I'll remain unaffected. If they really thought I was just terrible with people and didn't have skills or whatever, that would be a different issue. Then I'd have to think, "Maybe I need to be a priest in a different context."

What were John's greatest problems during his first years of priesthood?

I don't know that I would qualify anything as a problem. I would say, a frustration. I am frustrated by a lack of leadership. Every parish is a denomination unto itself in a lot of ways, meaning the diversity that does not fit within the scheme of being Catholic. There is too much a mark of every individual pastor in a lot of ways. But the hierarchical constitution is divine. It's the will of Christ. So if it's the will of Christ, let's exercise it. We have one of the top five popes of all time. We have a bishop who is an outstanding man. And too often that Pope's words will never get to the parish level, because there is something in the middle frustrating those effects. It is priests who don't believe what the Church teaches and don't recognize the authority of the Pope and the bishop.

What does John hope for in his future?

I would like to spend some period of my life in an environment where being faithful to the Church is what is expected of you rather than something that is held as suspect and forces you to the margins. Maybe in one of the new religious orders. God wants faithful priests everywhere, and there is no such thing as a place where your priesthood can't bring about good.

Ninety percent of the people in the pews want real Catholicism in its full measure. And they haven't been getting it in a long time, and I think church attendance reflects that. They want the catechism and not just carefully selected elements. The real presence of the Eucharist. There really is a hell. There really is sin. There really is virtue. There really is grace and true charity. The glory of the saints. The wealth of writings and spiritual treatises we have to offer. Simply the breadth of two thousand years of Catholicism. Simply the whole gamut. Build the churches that you tore down in the seventies. Find the statues that you threw away. Give people Catholic piety again. Have the humility to learn from the places that are thriving. Lincoln, Nebraska, is thriving, whether you like Bishop _____ or not. Legionaries can't build their seminaries fast enough. And simply reconsider what is really happening rather than what they thought should have been happening through the eighties.

Chapter 4

Four Types of Resigned Priests

Now we turn our attention to resigned priests, and we begin with the most obvious question: Why did they leave? The reasons vary. The best way to communicate the major motivations inducing priests to resign is to identify types of resignees. If this is done well, it conveys the varieties of resignees and the circumstances impelling them to leave.

We used all our resources to carry out the task: 72 phone interviews, 13 personal interviews, and many observations by persons not directly connected with our study. All the information was on resigned priests who were ordained in 1992 or later.

Any categorization must emphasize some factors and neglect others. Our categorization is based on the priests' major motivations for leaving. We found that most resignees had two levels of motivation: one, a feeling of loneliness or being unappreciated; two, an additional situation or event that precipitated a crisis of commitment. Both are needed to bring about a resignation; either level taken alone is not enough. Using the two-level model, we identified four types of resigned priests in our data, plus an "other" category into which we put several unusual cases.

Type 1: In Love. A heterosexual priest felt lonely or unappreciated, and he fell in love. (About 20 to 30 percent of all resigned priests.)

Type 2: Rejected Celibacy. A heterosexual priest felt lonely or unappreciated, and he decided he could not continue as a celibate; no specific woman is involved. (About 20 to 30 percent.)

Type 3: Disillusioned. A heterosexual or homosexual priest felt lonely or unappreciated and was disillusioned by experiences with fellow priests or the Church hierarchy since ordination. (About 30 to 40 percent.)

Type 4: Rejected Gay Celibacy. A homosexual priest felt lonely or unappreciated, and he wanted an open, long-term relationship with a man. He rejected the option of living a double life. (About 5 to 15 percent.)

Other. Cases that do not fit the major four types. (About 5 to 10 percent.)

An important lesson here is that all four types have one condition in common— that the man felt lonely or unappreciated. This is a necessary requirement in the process of deciding to resign; when it is absent, resignation from the priesthood is unlikely. Whether a priest is heterosexual or homosexual, in love or not, it will not drive him to resign unless at the same time he feels lonely or unappreciated. This is a basic finding of our research.

Some examples of the types are presented below. All their stories are real-life; the quotations are taken from the interviews. To preserve anonymity, the names of individuals, the names of religious orders, and other details have been changed.

Type 1: In Love

Tom: Overcome by the Power of Love

Tom is a clear example of a priest who found himself in love. He grew up in a small town in the Midwest, the youngest of four children. He went to the nearby state university, where he got a degree in math education, hoping to be a teacher and coach.

While in college he became active in the Newman Center and grew close to Father Dan, a priest at the center. During this time there was no talk of going to seminary, but in his senior year Tom did discuss it with Father Dan.

> He approached me. I didn't bring up the topic, although I think it was in the back of my mind. He brought it up to me. . . . We were in daily conversation. We played golf together. I would stop in his office on the way home from school, and it was one of those conversations. I sat down and we were shooting the breeze. I was about to leave to do student teaching. I think I was talking to him about the struggles, like, "Yeah, I'm doing student teaching, but I don't want to be a teacher." He asked me if I ever thought about the priesthood. At that time in the back of my head I think I had. The question was, "What is it like?"

> I really enjoyed Dan. I enjoyed our friendship and looked at what he was doing at the Newman Center. I thought, "God, I like doing this stuff. So that's a possibility." So that triggered the idea. Father Dan contacted the diocesan vocation director. I met with him, and he was enthusiastic. Soon I was filling out the papers.

Interviewer: "Were you dating anyone at this time?"

Not seriously. Just casually. It wasn't one person. I didn't date a lot. It was more friendship dating.

Interviewer: "What tipped you toward seminary and away from teaching?"

I can't say one particular thing, other than really evaluating what I enjoyed doing. Looking at the math and education courses I was taking, I was just going through the motions. But my activity at the Newman Center, I wasn't just going through the motions there. I thoroughly enjoyed it. I was good at it. I got great positive reinforcement there. I wasn't going through the motions there.

Tom entered a university-related seminary in the East.

I liked it. I got to experience a university campus. The seminary at the time was going through a major transition. I had to go to pre-theology, because I had not had theology in college. The first year there I was in pre-theology. There were problems at the seminary, and while I was there, many students exited. The seminary had a reputation of being a vanguard, always on the forefront of things. Something happened, and the bishops started to pull the reins in a bit. That frustrated the formation faculty. The seminary had a reputation for having gays. It was heavily populated by homosexuals, and some were active. The bishops started to crunch down on that, and that caused all kinds of divisions. Some bishops were pulling guys out, and some guys just left.

The tensions started to build. We had a division, for lack of better terms, between conservative versus liberal. That division really started to play itself out not only in the formation faculty but in the student population. It was a mess. I didn't know anything about seminary training when I got there. I got thrown into this mix, where you have, for lack of better terms, conservatives and liberals fighting each other, and I'm exposed to it all.

Back home my parish was not progressive. The priest there was a good, solid guy. My experience of him was a guy walking around in street clothes. Then I went to seminary and you had these far-conservative guys walking around in cassocks. I'm like "What the hell is that?" All this stuff was going on.

My diocese put me there because they thought I could handle it academically and everything else. I delved into it. I was trying to figure it out. And I wasn't getting swayed one way or the other. I was enjoying the university. I was getting a great education. I ate it up. I was like a sponge. The Scripture studies, Church history, I took it at its best. I was enjoying it. I was in the middle of the road and could look at both sides. The really conservative people were taking a stance and ignoring some of the Church history. The really liberal people were using Scripture and Church history to bash the conservatives. I'm like, "Why are you doing that?" I was level-headed, and I think that's why the diocese kept me there.

I developed five really close friends my first year in pre-theology. The class of pre-theologians, there were five of us. But when we got to first-year theology, there were like thirty. In the first-year class there was a major division. Some were walking around in cassocks and really romanticizing the pre-Vatican II Church and whatnot. You had other guys on the other end of the spectrum. There were five of us who developed a friendship and said, "This is crazy. We'll support each other and plow through."

Interviewer: "What happened to the five guys?"

This is a sad story. Only two of us were ordained. The others left one by one. They were good guys who had made well-thought-out decisions. All that remained were a very good friend of mine and myself.

Interviewer: "How did you deal with the whole gay thing?"

It was something new. I did know one person before who was gay, but I didn't know he was gay until after I was in the seminary. In the seminary, my guess would be that forty or fifty percent were homosexual. The rule was that you could be a homosexual, but if you were at all active, you're out of there. That was their rule. Any activity at all and you were gone. I think I handled it well in the sense of not judging people. If you are having sex as a homosexual, you are an active homosexual and should not be there. If not, okay. You are preparing to be a celibate priest. If you are active in the seminary heterosexually, maybe seminary is not the place for you. That was my approach. Not that I made good friends with people who I knew were homosexual, not because they were homosexual but because we were different.

Looking back today, Tom praised his seminary courses, his fieldwork, and his summers ministering in his home diocese. After five years he was ordained and returned home. He was 31 years old. His first assignment was in an unattractive parish whose pastor was also new. Tom already knew the pastor, Dave. Both were young. So the two of them went there together and had a "hell of a time" bringing the parish back to life. It was a great experience. Tom and Dave were full of energy.

We got new blood in there. People got fired up. We remodeled the church, pulled the pews out. We stripped and stained them. We got new carpet. Church attendance increased. It was fun. I enjoyed it.

Tom worked hard to develop a youth group based on two parishes. It thrived. Soon they had a Mass for teenagers at six on Sunday evenings, plus a music group. At the first youth Mass they had two hundred teenagers. The growing youth program received wide publicity, and Tom felt proud.

At the end of the first year the bishop pulled Dave out and sent in Father Frank, a totally different pastor. Frank was 66 years old, at the end of a career in small, one-man parishes in farming communities. In Tom's opinion he was not prepared for this urban parish, which had a thousand families, an RCIA team, and an associate.

> That was my second year, 1995. This guy was out of his element, but a nice guy. I felt sorry for him. We had conflicts. He was not used to an RCIA team, and he didn't trust it. He was not happy. That year was not a fun year, and I was partly to blame. We had all these activities going on, and I didn't want them to end. We were remodeling, building an extension on to the church. We were working with the finance council, and we had a contractor and architect. That was before Frank came into the picture. So when there were problems or decisions needed in all this, they came to me. In retrospect I should have sent them to Frank. He was upset about that. That caused tension. And other little things. With the youth group, I had a group of twenty young adults my age working with this youth group. They became my friends. You don't see that in church often. So I had friends, some were married, some single. They were very involved. People were coming in and out of the rectory during the day. It was fun. They'd call me Tom. "Hey Tom, what are you doing?" But Frank is old school, and you call him "Father Altevogt." My friend came in and said "Hi Frank" to him, and all hell broke loose. You don't call him that. That put a damper on that group of people.

The parish situation deteriorated, and the bishop stepped in. Tom was given a new assignment as a part-time teacher in a Catholic school, part-time associate in a different parish. He lived at the school.

> When I moved out of the parish to [the school], I was really isolated, because it was just me in an apartment. It was about five miles from the school, not convenient for people to drop by. It was a strange year, and it was no fun.

> During that time one of the women involved in the music youth group at the parish, she and I became very good friends. She is now my wife. She was in a religious community and was our liturgist. She was a huge help for me in planning youth liturgies. We started doing things together. Soon I know I'm really attracted to her, I knew I'm over my head. I'm spending time with her. It was a mutual attraction. Now I'm calling my friend who is a priest in Pennsylvania. I'm calling him and saying "I'm in trouble." Well, not in trouble, but it was new territory for me.

> He came to visit me. We talked, and I talked to her. I told her, "I'm new in the priesthood and I love what I do. I'm not ready to throw that away. But I can't stay here." So I called the bishop and said, "I'm in a relationship and I'm not handling it well. I need to get out of town." So he moved me at once to [Blessed Sacrament] in a suburb across the state. This caused all sorts of speculation in the diocese, because it's a mid-year move, and I was the only one moved.

Now Tom was near where his parents lived. Did they know about the woman?

They're picking it up. I didn't tell them until the move. I need to tell you that Mom and Dad got very excited to have a son who was a priest. My brother was hugely excited, but my sisters were like, "What the hell are you doing? Are you sure you want to do this?" But after I was ordained they were very supportive.

And this youth group in _____ was going very well. It was getting diocesan attention; our pictures were in the paper; we were on the news. So when I got sent to Blessed Sacrament, my parents knew that a woman was involved. Now I was struggling. I was depressed.

Interviewer: "Did you go into counseling?"

I started counseling with a Jesuit there. He was very good.

Interviewer: "Was the bishop aware of the struggle you were going through?"

Yes, aware and supportive. He did everything he could. But the parish he put me in, Blessed Sacrament, was not good for me. He really had no other alternative. The parish is an old-money, conservative parish with a pastor who was out there on the far right of things. Anyone who knows him and me knew that it was not a good match. So I started working with the people, working with the RCIA, and I enjoyed my time there on top of my struggles and my depression. I struggled with the pastor. We were just different, not good or bad, just different. So I didn't do much with him.

After about three months I'm plugging along at Blessed Sacrament. No contact with Joan, who was still in _____. Mom and Dad came to my parish for Sunday and daily Mass. They asked me, "Why aren't you happy?" I'm like, "I'm not in a place where I am happy." I had a lot of stuff going on.

That spring, four months after I came to Blessed Sacrament, I break down and contact Joan. I call her.

Interviewer: "Why do you say it was a breakdown?"

Because my whole goal was to separate myself from her. That was my goal when I asked for the transfer. I told the bishop I was involved in a relationship, and it was my intent to separate. He didn't make me promise that, but that was what I was to work on. I missed Joan. She had a beautiful voice, a beautiful liturgist. Blessed Sacrament was an old-time church where you have the altar way up here, all the people back there. It is a beautiful church, but not my style of liturgy. Nothing like we had in _____. This was kind of a downer for me. It was not my view of what a Catholic parish should be, but that's what a lot of parishes are. The people come to church for one hour and are rushing to get out of the parking lot.

Interviewer: "When you contacted Joan, what did you say?"

It was good to talk to her. I started off by apologizing and then talked to her about what Blessed Sacrament was like. "You won't believe what is going on! We have nuns running around in full habit." I was like, "I can't believe it, they are in full habit. It's just crazy." It was just a general conversation, but we agreed to stay in contact. During the summer we arranged to meet each other halfway. We were two hours away from each other, and we met in the middle. That became a routine of meeting about once every two weeks. I'm in counseling, and I tell my counselor what has happened. He's supportive. He said, "Maybe Joan should see someone." My counselor saw us together twice.

By now we're seeing each other twice a week. No one knows. At the end of the summer I'm like, "This has got to stop." I put a stop to seeing Joan and tried to throw myself into the church. But I was not happy. I was depressed, still in counseling. I'm not doing anything with the pastor. We lived in the same house and hardly ever saw each other.

Interviewer: "What caused you to decide something had to change?"

A bad incident. I became sexually involved with a woman at Blessed Sacrament. This was not the relationship that I wanted. It was not right. I was not seeing Joan, but I realized that she was what I wanted. By now it was fall. I increased counseling and talked to the bishop again. I told him that I really screwed up this time and was thinking about a leave of absence. I soon ended the relationship with the woman. The bishop agreed that he would give me a leave of absence, but he asked if I could wait until June. So I continued till June.

I made the announcement of my leave in June. I told my parents in February, and they knew before the announcement. They were upset but also were worried because I was depressed. Came June, I made the announcement and did not know what I was going to do.

The bishop wanted me out of town, and he wanted me to continue counseling. He had connections in [city to the north], so I moved up here, hooked up with a counselor, and got a job teaching in a Catholic high school. I stayed there a year, living in the basement of a rectory for a while. Then I moved out and got an apartment.

By now Joan knew about the relationship with the other woman and that I was on leave of absence. She left her community at about this time and started working for a degree at [a Catholic university]. She was angry at me for what I did, but there was no contact. I'm up here teaching and she's in college. She's there, I'm here, no contact. I'm still depressed. I want to talk to her. I go on a mad scramble to find e-mail addresses of students at the university. I got her e-mail address and e-mailed her totally out of the blue. Then I was depressed because she did not respond for a couple of weeks. Finally she responded via e-mail. We e-mailed back and forth for a while and finally decided to get together and talk.

I was in contact with my bishop, because I was still on a leave of absence. The bishop and another priest came up twice to see me. They met with the counselor, and we did group sessions. Soon Joan and I were seeing each other again. I also saw that teaching wasn't my ball of wax, and I was looking for a different job. I ended up working for Catholic Service, coordinating volunteers. I'm still there. Joan moved up here, and I told the bishop I would not be coming back. I told my parents that I was ending my connection with the diocese. They announced in the paper that summer that I had resigned.

Interviewer: "When did you and Joan get married?"

We've been married one year. It was two years after I left the diocese. It was a long struggle. We lived in the same town, we dated. After I made the decision not to go back to the diocese, I told her, "I'm not going back to the priesthood, therefore I'm going to marry you."

All that was hard on my parents: my resigning, my taking a leave of absence. When I left the diocese and moved here, I was very depressed, to the point that they worried about me hurting myself, because I didn't know anyone. When I kind of got on my feet, the worry subsided, but the hurt and anger on my dad's part for leaving the priesthood is still there.

Interviewer: "Did they come to your wedding?"

Barely. Mom is such a loving, caring person. Dad is a stoic German. I don't think he would have come, but Mom said, "You are going to the wedding." And they came. Before we were married, Joan and I went to visit them. The first time we were in the house together, my dad did not acknowledge Joan. That was a struggle for us. What could we do? But Mom convinced Dad to accept her.

Joan's family was easier. They already knew me. I knew her sisters, her mom and dad, and her brother before I knew her. They are fine with the marriage. They even helped with the wedding.

Interviewer: "Where are you at with the Church now?"

We are still active in the Church. I applied for laicization. The bishop was supportive. I was doing that somewhat for myself but a lot for my parents, so I wasn't going to be crestfallen if it got rejected. They sent it off, and it got rejected. Actually the case itself didn't get rejected, it didn't even get looked at. They sent it back to the bishop saying, "We won't look at it until he's forty years old." I was like, "I'm not going to let that stop us. I can't wait until I'm forty years old. I'm thirty-six now." So we planned to get married.

I told Mom and Dad that I was applying for laicization, but that it didn't come through and we were going to get married anyway. That was a catastrophe in Dad's eyes. My mom was crestfallen about me getting married outside the Church.

Now we are active in our parish. Joan does music, and I preach every once in a while. I talked to the pastor and asked if we could use the church for the wedding. He had no problem with that. We hooked up with a friend who is an Episcopalian priest. Nice guy. He agreed to preside, so we had an Episcopalian priest and got married in our own parish.

We are still active in the Church. We receive Communion. Joan is very strong that if you go to church, you receive Communion. My mom and dad think we are very outside of the Church and cannot receive Communion. Dad would throw a fit if he saw us receiving Communion. But the priest at our parish has no problems with giving us Communion. And the other priests who know me give me Communion.

Interviewer: "Would you like to be a married priest if that were possible?"

People ask me that. My initial thought was yes. I loved doing what I did as a priest. Preaching, presiding. You get involved in people's lives in a unique way. But now when people ask me that, I say no, because I am angry at the Church, angry and hurt. I'm confused as to where it is going. I knew this as an active minister, that there are almost two Churches—the people, then the hierarchy. You get these pronouncements that almost say "No salvation outside of the Church." I love the Catholic tradition, because to me it works. I love the sacraments. It builds my relationship with God. I'm Catholic even if the Catholic Church tells me I'm not. That's hurtful, because to me I'm Catholic.

Type 2: Rejected Celibacy

Carl: Can't Stand the Loneliness

Carl rejected celibate living but without a powerful love affair pulling on him, and he exemplifies a large number of resignees. Carl grew up in a working-class German family in a small town in Illinois. He had nine siblings and an alcoholic father.

Dad, even with all of his difficulties with alcoholism, he was still a devout Catholic. He would pray his rosary, and he'd have his cards all lined up, his prayer cards, in front of him. He had them in a shoebox, and there was hell to pay if anyone got them out of order. Whenever he walked by the crucifix he would kiss the feet of the Corpus, Jesus. With all the turbulence in our childhood, the Church was one sure strength in our family. And the parish priest had been there about as long as I could remember.

Carl was socially shy during high school. He got good grades and tried to fit in. He felt sorry for his mother, raising the family.

> I saw all the stuff that Mom went through and almost single-handedly rais-
> ing ten kids. I had a great deal of empathy for her and her struggle. The other
> kids, they kind of went their own way, and I felt sorry for Mom being left in
> a situation like this. So there was a special relationship between us, I think.

Carl went to a state college and got a degree in engineering. He wasn't
especially interested in engineering, but he was good at math and science,
and a guidance counselor in high school suggested it. So he gave it a try.
Carl reflected that early in life he let other people make decisions for him.

> One of the patterns of my life is, I have a lot of other people make my deci-
> sions for me. Not being very self-confident, and I had a fairly low self-
> image. Like I said, I didn't date a lot. I allowed many other people to make
> decisions for me. The guidance counselor basically put an idea in my mind
> about computer engineering. It was like, "Okay." I would have liked to have
> been a teacher. But back then I remember Mom saying that you couldn't
> support a family being a teacher.

Interviewer: "When did you begin thinking about becoming a priest?"

> From Mom saying things when I was small, to being socially awkward in
> high school, not being very good at dating. And when Dad died when I was
> in college, that was certainly influential. That really shook up my life, be-
> cause it was the first death I'd experienced.

Carl went to work for a computer firm and did well. He earned good
money, but he was troubled by the meaninglessness of his work.

> I put my life and heart and soul into this one computer program, months of my
> life, and I delivered it to the company. And I said, "There." And I got to think-
> ing, "So what? What difference does it make in anybody's life?" And I remem-
> ber thinking, looking at Dad's tombstone, what would I like to have written on
> my tombstone? And I started having a crisis of meaning in what I was doing.

Carl saw an article in the parish bulletin inviting anyone to visit a seminary and check it out. It was a "come and see" program. He went and found
the people to be extremely human and lively. "Very real, not unlike me."
He took a leave of absence from his job and went to seminary for a year.
He loved it.

> My first year at seminary was absolutely wonderful. I loved learning about
> the faith, more about my Church, Church history, Scripture, all those things.
> It was an eye-opening experience, my first real formal education in regard to
> anything theological. Before seminary I had been pretty isolated. I had a
> bunch of friends, which was great, but I think I maybe dated one person one
> time in two years. So going into this community where there were all these
> guys, it was actually a very fun experience.

I needed to do some pre-theology in order to enter graduate school of theology. So there were about thirty of us in pre-theology, people with masters degrees and teachers, and from all around the country. It was a very interesting group of people. One of the things I found out is that about half of them were adult children of alcoholics, me being one. And I had no idea what ACOA [Adult Children of Alcoholics] was, and I started reading some books and went through some counseling. I basically started to deal with the issues of childhood, some of the hurt, the anger, how it affected me.

For theology, Carl chose a free-standing seminary in the Midwest. He loved it, and meanwhile he struggled with the issue of celibacy.

I had been celibate my whole life, didn't know anything different. Never dated a whole lot. You know, how difficult could the celibacy thing be? I've lived it all my life so far, how hard could it be? I don't know that I realized how socially inhibited I was. I wasn't real confident in my abilities or in my looks.

In his second year he felt lonely and considered taking a leave of absence from the seminary, but the vocational director persuaded him to stay and to take an intern year in a parish. He agreed. During that year in a parish he got involved romantically with a woman.

Not a whole lot developed from it, but I decided that wasn't for me. I decided to go back to the seminary, sort of to get away from her. I still didn't know what I wanted to do.

Carl told of his fieldwork experiences and his intern year. He spoke glowingly about the good experiences, but at the same time he said he felt lonely that year.

In the third year Carl needed to start planning his diaconate ordination.

And I felt like I was on a train but didn't know how to get off of it. I didn't have the wherewithal, the courage, the self-image, or, I think, the support to say, "Whoa, I'm not ready for this."

I think, being an adult child of an alcoholic, I was a people-pleaser. I did my studies, I was a responsible person. And I think people thought, "That would be a good priest." But I don't think anybody really challenged me, saying, "Are you sure you want to do this?" And I wish somebody had done that for me, to challenge me more and more that way.

I didn't know what I wanted to do. I felt like I was on this speeding train. I felt the urge to get off, but I felt I didn't have the wherewithal to get off. It almost felt like it was an addiction, this approval. I was almost addicted to this approval that I was getting, the attention, the approval. Suddenly I was somebody.

The interviewer asked Carl about preparation for celibacy during seminary.

> I think living in the seminary is not a real good test of living a celibate life. For heterosexuals, you are around guys all the time. If there is a woman in chapel, you're very much aware that there is a woman in chapel. I don't think it is a very realistic environment for seminarians to test celibacy. I'm not sure what to do about that, other than to have more experiences with the general public, where you mingle among them, where you build relationships with them. Have them exposed to more women. We had celibacy and sexuality workshops, but I don't remember them being particularly helpful.

> CPE [clinical pastoral training] was a good experience. That was a good way of dealing with some of the issues lurking back there. I did that before my internship, and it helped surface some issues.

In spite of his doubts and struggles, Carl was ordained in 1993. Even to the day of ordination he felt uneasy.

> I remember even on the day of priesthood ordination thinking, "What am I doing?" One of my best friends in seminary was a year ahead of me, and we were very close. He went through a struggle whether to go through with ordination or not. I remember him saying, "Hey, if I'm doing it, you're doing it." And as pathetic as it sounds, that put a lot of pressure on me to go through with it, with one of my best friends saying this.

> My first year of ministry was like a honeymoon in many ways. The pastor was very good, he was twenty years older than I was. He was fun, very communal, a good guy. He didn't like to deal with dirty stuff, meaning struggles or issues. He just wanted people to get along and to have fun. I think he had very high expectations of the people who worked at his parish. He was all about team ministry, but I think he was more about us being workhorses. He had an expectation that we'd work a minimum of fifty hours a week. That didn't help anything. Communally, it was great. We prayed Morning Prayer most mornings, sometimes we prayed Night Prayer. It was a healthy thing, and I enjoyed my years there in many ways.

> We lived at the rectory, where the offices were in the front and we lived in back. And he tried to do what he could to keep it separate, the business up front and the social in back. I don't think it is a healthy environment to work in. In some ways you're always on call. Someone is always ringing the doorbell. There are people walking around. We shared a kitchen with other people. So it was sort of living where you work. I think that contributed to some of the burnout that I felt.

Carl was in that parish for four years.

> Socially, it was good. Communally, there was a good community in the house, just the two of us. We had seminarians a couple of those years. That added to

it in some ways. There was certainly loneliness, no doubt about it. The people at the parish were excellent. It was almost an ideal situation except for the living conditions and the unrealistic expectations of the pastor.

Carl felt a sense of heaviness and of being somehow left behind. He became close to some families in the parish and envied their family life. Soon he got involved with a woman.

> It was in my second year after ordination, I think. I am embarrassed about it. I know it was wrong. I think it was more a symptom of what I was going through, the loneliness. I got involved sexually. A very unhealthy relationship. I ended up breaking it off. And I sought some counseling a couple of times through my spiritual director. One counselor said, "The priesthood isn't easy." One of the things he does with his wife is, he holds his wife twenty minutes at night when they go to sleep and twenty minutes in the morning when they wake up, and that's a very fulfilling thing. He said, "I don't know how a priest can live his life." This guy would have been a priest he if could have.

> I crossed boundaries as a priest because I wanted to get that being embraced. When does a hug get too long? At some point my desire was to be held, not to have a sexual relationship. And at times I crossed the line. The women would interpret the embrace as something different than what I wanted it to be. So I struggled with the issue of celibacy. I had maybe two sexual relationships when I was a priest. I'm embarrassed about that.

Time passed. Carl's father had died, his favorite priest from the home parish had died, and he felt less pressure to stay in the priesthood. After two sexual relationships, he decided he wanted to be married.

> I wanted to have someone in my life who is going to hold me accountable, who will just plain hold me and be there for me and with me. It's very unnatural to not have that consistent partner in life to challenge me, to hold me, to encourage me, to affirm me, to kick me in the butt periodically. Marriage can't be some of those things, obviously. It's not all of that. But the loneliness. I went into counseling. This was like the second or third counselor I'd seen while I was a priest. And now I started to think, "I can't continue the struggle. It's just too hard."

Carl was filled with doubts and questions. He went to a counselor who was himself a former priest.

> He was very helpful for me in helping deal with the issues at hand. I think people need people to be there for them and with them in the name of God. I wanted that. Whatever that meant, that was my dream. Do you have to be a priest to do that? I would like to believe you don't, that it's not the only vocation to do that. I think you can do that as a single person or as a married person. I'd like to be married to someone who will accompany me through this life.

Carl decided he couldn't go on. He told his pastor that he was thinking about taking a leave of absence.

> There was a lot of fulfillment in what I was doing, but there was a real emptiness too. And I found myself getting burned out. I starting to find myself getting cynical. My prayer life was starting to get really cold. And I was starting to realize that priesthood was suddenly killing me in my own spiritual life. And I don't think I'm rationalizing when I say that what is most important in a person's life is their relationship with the Lord. And you have to do what you have to do to take care of that relationship with God. Even if that means leaving the priesthood.

Carl left and returned to his computer job. He was 34 years old. He was invited back by the boss and soon was making good money, but he was restless. He decided he would like to be a counselor, and he left his job to take a master's degree in counseling in a nearby university. Just after leaving the priesthood he also started dating a woman, but unfortunately after two years she broke up with him.

Now Carl works as a counselor in a Catholic high school. He sees it as a meaningful ministry and hopes to work in schools in education in the future.

Does Carl miss being a priest?

> I sometimes miss presiding. But I don't miss the work schedule. I don't miss always being on call, and when there is always one more parishioner to visit. There is always somebody at the hospital. I didn't deal well with that. I'm something of a perfectionist, and I like closure. It was always very difficult for me to deal with, that my work was never ended. You can always put more time into your homily on Sunday. It was never ending. And I think it ended up burning me out.

How important was the desire to marry in Carl's decision to resign?

> Eighty to ninety percent. Certainly the workload was also a part of it, there is no doubt about that. I was getting burned out, and my faith struggle was getting greater with time. There was a coldness and feeling that I don't want to be doing this any more. I was losing the passion. That was certainly a strong element of it. But by and large it was the loneliness, the intense loneliness. That would be the main reason, that I wanted to be married, I wanted a spiritual partner in life, someone to hold me accountable, somebody who would walk with me in the name of God. And share my life.

Now Carl is busy in the high school and working on the laicization process. He hopes to become either a high school counselor or a private Christian counselor. For several months he has been dating a divorced woman, and she is working on her annulment. He hopes that the annulment will come and that they will marry in the Church. They are waiting.

Type 3: Disillusioned

We spoke at length with several priests of Type 3, but we don't have space to fully present one here. All the resignees of this type complained of impossible pastors in their first assignments or of irregularities they discovered.

For example, a young diocesan priest told about his parish:

> I was worried about my survival as a person! I was put in charge of everything. I was soon too busy and overworked. On top of that, I had no idea how to take care of myself, and I started being terribly unhappy and depressed. The older priests had no sympathy. Their attitude was, "We went through hell and you need to do it too." The priest culture seemed to be, "Just do it and shut up. No whining." I felt too much pressure to do everything, and my superiors didn't help. I felt thrown into everything at once. There was nobody I could talk to, and I could not go on.

Another young diocesan priest:

> I had an extremely poor experience in my priestly life. While I loved my ministry and the people I ministered to, I felt no support from the pastor. I lived with it. He was a man with no morals and a lot of profanity. He was an alcoholic, and he had an affair with a married parishioner. Having to live with a man like that was terrible.

Another:

> I saw myself at a dead end as one of the youngest in the diocese. It looked as if I would be only a sacramental functionary in the future. I was well educated, but nobody had an interest in making use of that. I see the same kind of thing across the country. My job was really stressful. I was in one of the better parishes, and I saw only downward movement for myself after that.

> There was a big divide among the priests according to sexual orientation. In clergy gatherings there was a clear line between the gays and the straights. It was the same in the seminary. Now it seems to be the question of whether the gays can be openly gay or not. This is a powder-keg issue. But because there is such a large gay bloc and because the Church doesn't want to deal with it, it makes discussion impossible.

Type 4: Rejected Gay Celibacy

Marc: Wanted to Live with Integrity

Gay priests experience unique stresses, as exemplified by Marc. He grew up in a French-Canadian family in New England. His family was religiously active, and his uncle was a diocesan priest. Marc was small when this uncle died, and he remembers the funeral. The bishop presided.

> At the funeral this bishop wanted to express his condolences to the immediate family. And then when he met me, I remember he actually put his hand on my head and said, "I think someday you'll take your uncle's place in the priesthood," as if I was preordained at that time. . . . I think that is actually part of my story of how I ended up going into the Franciscans and being ordained, and yet discovering later that it was a mistake. Maybe I was doing it for other people rather than for myself. And I think part of that story is that my father was once in the seminary but left.

Marc explained that his father's brother had committed suicide when he was fourteen years old, and the family felt rejected. The church didn't have a funeral Mass for him, and the family felt a sense of shame that lasted for years.

> And the idea was maybe if we could produce a priest, it would redeem the family from the shame of this suicide. And my father was going to do that, but then he fell in love with my mother and that didn't pan out. So I was the next one that came along. It was kind of like the family story had a niche carved out for me and I slipped into it without really figuring it out. From the age of about five or six, I can remember playing priest at home. And my parents would encourage this. I played like a priest presiding at Mass. In fact, I had an aunt who was a cloistered nun in Canada; she made a mini-set of vestments for me. [Laugh.] Even as a kid, it was like I had a little niche, and my family did not discourage it.

Marc went to Catholic high school. At college he majored in religious studies and theology, thinking about having a career either in religion or in international work. During college he became interested in world religions and immersed himself in Buddhism and Islam. Also he met some impressive Franciscan priests.

> The priests weren't living in the dormitories, but I had some in class and got acquainted with others through attending Sunday church services. I was very attracted to the liberation theology undertone to a lot of their work and their social justice focus. That's what really got me excited about the possibility of ministry, because it seemed to combine both that faith perspective with fundamental values about service, plus the idea of looking at the whole world. This was the time in the late seventies, when there was a lot of stuff going on in Central America with liberation theology. I was reading books by Paulo Freire, Leonardo Boff, and Gustavo Gutierrez. And these people serving the government of Nicaragua at the time. I remember the Pope came and scolded them. There were two priest brothers. I was really interested in this stuff.

In thinking about the priesthood, Marc preferred religious orders, because diocesan priesthood looked too confining.

I found the Franciscans to be a refreshing counterforce to what I saw as these forces of silence and oppression within the Church. And I thought, "Hey, I want to be part of this movement towards liberalization and openness and change." And I knew immediately that if I was ever going to do ministry in the Church, it should be as a Franciscan. I wouldn't be able to do it within the structure of dioceses; that would be too limiting.

After graduating, Marc taught for a year, and meanwhile he took part in retreats and discernment programs. He still felt called to the priesthood, so he resigned his teaching job after one year and entered a seminary. He studied philosophy the first year, then did a novitiate as a high school teacher. He entered seminary and thoroughly enjoyed it. He had recurring doubts about the faith, but several faculty members whom he admired counseled him to persevere. He was seeing a psychotherapist the whole time. After seminary he earned a master's degree in counseling in the East while working part-time in a parish. He was ordained at the age of 34. About this time he became troubled by loneliness, partly because he was living in institution-like surroundings. He began seeing a therapist again, and soon he felt a desire to move to the San Francisco area, where the atmosphere was more liberal. Yet moving there did not solve the problems.

All these things were coming together. Namely, my family stuff, with the divorce of my parents and its toll on my mother. Even though I made the best decision that I could at that time, I was partly trying to please my family and fulfill this family function of redeeming the family. I didn't really choose it myself, I was kind of chosen for it. And then I was doing more with my sexuality and sexual feelings. I came out as a gay man. And then I realized, "Well geez, I think I might want to be in a relationship. If I stay in this structure I have to hide, and not really make myself available to do that." So quite a few factors came together.

I loved being a Franciscan, I loved the community stuff, I loved the work, loved the studies. In one sense, the clincher for me was becoming aware that I couldn't do the priest thing, and that was after I was ordained. I don't know that there was any way of knowing it until after I was ordained. Because what happened for me is that ordination propelled me into this role that I never really had that much experience with before, namely, the role of being a representative of the institutional Church and presiding at liturgies and preaching. Before that I was doing social work, I was teaching liberation theology in the classroom, I was doing all the things that were okay for me. But then there was just so much conflict over the real me versus what the Church was doing. I could kind of skirt around it when I was in these other positions, but I couldn't skirt around it when I was in the role. And even when it came to presiding in sacraments or when people came for reconciliation, they are confessing sins that I don't think are offenses against God.

And I felt like I needed to be true to myself, but then that would confuse people. It just got to be too much of a mess. Being myself and being in this role just didn't fit.

But it was as if, until I was in that role, I couldn't really know that completely. I could know it intellectually, but I didn't know it in my gut. So I struggled for several years to try and make it work, but finally I gave up. It was like wearing a costume that I didn't want to wear, to put it in a Halloween metaphor.

Marc told about one of his seminary professors who was a gay priest.

Here was this guy, John _____, who was liberal. He was happy, he was out as a gay man, and he was out in his ministerial life, and he made it work. And I thought, "Oh, maybe I can be like John." So I had these role models that showed me that even with the conflicts I was having, it was possible to stay a Franciscan and deal with all these things. So I kind of kept going, trying to see if I could make that happen for myself. But once I started grad school, I realized that it's not working.

In the Franciscan community there was an explicit "It's okay to be 'out' in here, but don't be 'out' out there." When John was "out" in his ministry as a teacher, he could go into a classroom and talk about being gay or whatever, but you don't go into a church on a weekend and preach from your experience from the pulpit or make pro-gay remarks. And it's not only that issue, but I remember when I did my preaching, I would try to make language more gender neutral, and it would upset people in the congregation. They'd say, "You're taking away our tradition." Or if I might make remarks about women's rights or gay rights or things like that, people would really get agitated. And I realized, this is not a good fit. I can't really be a spiritual leader for these people. I was a little too far out of the range of what people wanted in a leader to be good for that role.

Interviewer: "Wanting to have a partner and to be sexually engaged in life, was that a factor?"

Yeah. Part of the therapy was that I realized all these fears about intimacy that I had, how in some ways my going into the community was a way I could avoid dealing with my fears of intimacy and my sexuality. And that wasn't the only thing. In terms of being myself, I kind of went from college and then I was into the Franciscans, and I really never had the chance to be a grown-up, have my own place with my own things, and make a salary and make ends meet. I felt unless I had that experience and some kind of independence in the world, that I wasn't going to grow much any more. And so, in other words, it was more than just the issues around sexuality, it was also that I didn't want to be in this Franciscan community and have this vow of obedience and not have charge over my own life. It was more than just the priest thing, it was also some of the issues that were involved in being in a religious community.

Interviewer: "Like loss of autonomy?"

Yeah, exactly. And no possibility for, potentially, the kind of relationship that could be satisfying.

Interviewer: "Do you have a partner now?"

No. I'm dating someone, but we're not hooked up.

Marc did not start the dispensation process, since he saw no need for it. Better to keep all options open.

Interviewer: "Are you active now as a Catholic?"

I guess culturally I'm a Catholic. I don't practice regularly. I practice occasionally. I'm actually quite good friends with a Franciscan pastor I knew from before, so I go there once in a while, and we get together for dinner. He has a very liberal community. Maybe I'm back to my original exploring thing, because I worship in different churches and different communities, wandering around. [Laugh.] A man without a home.

Chapter 5

Life Experiences of Newly Ordained Active and Resigned Priests

Our project gave us abundant information about the past lives of newly ordained priests. For all human beings, early life experiences produce specific strengths and weaknesses in a person's personality, and they remain for life. Priests are a distinct category of person, and very likely many of them have had early life experiences different from the average. In addition, specific events after ordination affected subsequent priestly careers in often decisive ways. In this chapter we look into these two categories of experience—in early life and after ordination.

Regarding early life experiences, we wondered about two questions. First, did priests as a group have unique childhoods? Do men of certain personality types self-select themselves into the priesthood? Second, did specific childhood events develop tendencies in some of these men? Priests vary in coping style and resilience, as we saw clearly in our interviews. Under particular circumstances some priests feel demoralized or will even contemplate resignation; others, in identical circumstances, are unfazed in commitments and dedication. Our interviews provided some information about the childhoods of these priests.

Childhood Experiences

We heard a remarkable number of priests mention that they were sons of alcoholic fathers. Psychologists have done considerable research on adult children of alcoholics (called "ACOAs"). American society contains a surprisingly high number of ACOAs; one expert put the number at 20 million

(Page, 1991:7). The research shows that ACOAs frequently suffer from interpersonal problems that include anxiety about intimate relationships, emotional distancing, impulsive behavior, and constant need for approval (Johnson and Bennett, 1989; Martin, 1995). Children who grow up with an alcoholic parent, especially with an alcoholic father, are at high risk for substance abuse and problems with mood and anxiety disorders (Cuijpers et al., 1999). When relations in the family are unpredictable because of a parent's alcoholic behavior, children learn to anticipate mistrust in relationships, a condition that carries over into adult life. ACOAs may desire love and intimacy, but those desires are sometimes blocked by fears that a new adult relationship will be as troubled as were the family relationships when they were children.

We have no statistics on how many priests are children of alcoholics, but past researchers have noticed that Catholic priests are more often ACOAs than are average adults. From our research we have no proof of the effects of a childhood with an alcoholic parent, but based on research by psychologists, the problem is serious enough that seminary administrators should always be alert to the situation.[1] Here, for example, is a resigned diocesan priest:

> My father's alcoholism certainly influences who I am today, no doubt about it. It helped shape my personality. I don't say that as an excuse. I think there are reasons for who I am today, but I make my own choices. I think, being an adult child of an alcoholic, I was a people-pleaser. I just wanted people to get along, be happy. I was suddenly getting a lot of attention in seminary, lots of affirmation from people. Generally I was a good guy and people generally liked me. And I think people thought, "That would be a good priest." But I don't think anybody was supportive of challenging me to say, "Are you sure you want to do this?" And I wish somebody had done that for me, to challenge me more and more about doing that.

A very insightful resigned diocesan priest:

> I grew up in an alcoholic home that included a high degree of familial discord. As many people understand today, the effects of such unpredictability

---

[1] In 1972 Andrew Greeley tested the importance of childhood family problems on the probability that a priest will resign. He used his large 1970 study for this purpose and found definite relationships: "The hypothesis that a strain in family background will relate to resignation from the priesthood is supported by the studies. In every one of ten comparisons that can be made between resignees and actives, the resignees are more likely to report problems in the family background, and in some cases, the differences are quite substantial" (1972b, p. 32). The situation in 1970 is not quite the same as in 2001, and problems in family background include much more than alcoholism of parents. Thus the Greeley findings are suggestive but not conclusive about ACOAs today.

are profound. Children tend to have traits such as having a hard time being honest, learning to stifle feelings and needs, difficulty trusting others, and difficulty being emotionally close to others. I turned to God for help in managing a rather unmanageable situation, and I turned to the Church to find the surrogate parents and metaphorical home to make up for what was lacking in my own home.

A corollary of the theories about alcoholic fathers is that boys who grew up in alcoholic or otherwise tumultuous families tend to have overly close relations with their mothers. Indeed, past researchers have found that Catholic seminarians disproportionately have dominant mothers (Hoge et al., 1984:23). An older resigned diocesan priest told about his mother's reaction when he left the priesthood to marry:

It was hard for my mom. She had become a real "priest's mother." She got active in all the parishes wherever I was sent. It was hard for her. She lost a lot. But she reconciled herself a lot, and it was the best thing that ever happened to Mom. My sister said to me that now Mom has to share you with another woman. That's difficult for her.

A second theme of priesthood in our interviews was that some priests told of strong parental pressure for them to enter the priesthood. This pressure motivated them to become a priest, but anyone should expect, in the course of normal life, that as time passes and parents die, this motivation will disappear. Then the priest finds himself less committed. A resigned diocesan priest told of his experience:

I remember one time Mom said, with the youngest five boys in the car, "It would be really great if one of you guys ever wanted to be a priest." So the seed was sort of planted in me, in the sense of seeking Mom's approval. If I ever wanted Mom's approval, I would definitely want to become a priest. . . . A year after I graduated from college, my father died. I remember in that last year of his life, at some point he was in the hospital. One of the things he said in the last years of his life was that if I ever wanted to be a priest, he had fistfuls of money to educate me. That had a powerful impact on me.

A third theme mentioned by several priests was that as boys they were socially shy and afraid that girls did not like them. A few mentioned a fear of intimacy. Here is a topic not easy for anyone to discuss, let alone a priest, so probably this trait occurs much more often in reality than it did in our interviews. Nevertheless our interviewees did touch on the subject, often using a formula "I didn't date much." Here is an active diocesan priest:

I've always been somewhat of an independent soul, to the point that it seemed odd to other people. I could go to a movie alone and not feel uncomfortable, and my friends always thought that was so strange. So I always felt like it certainly wouldn't be unreasonable for me to be celibate. I was dating someone when I was twenty-two, a very sweet, nice girl. And I remember one time she had to go away for the weekend for a family thing. I remember I was just so happy! "Oh great, a weekend for myself! I'm going to read this and do this and that." And that was, maybe that was a sign.

A resigned diocesan priest:

In high school I didn't date a lot. I was socially very shy. I just wanted to fit in. I wanted to get along. I was one of the peacemakers. I was one of the good kids. I didn't cause any trouble. I got good grades. . . . I remember, one girl turned me down for a date and I thought, "Well, I'm just going to become a priest then." Sort of like, "Well, if I can't date anybody, I might as well become a priest."

A resigned diocesan priest reflected on his relationships while in seminary:

I enjoyed the friendship of male peers, with whom I could gradually risk deeper emotional closeness. Because there was not a sexual component to these relationships for me, they were safe and less threatening with regard to my fear of intimacy. In many ways the college and graduate seminary had a kind of "chum-like," adolescent-boy feeling, which was where I was personally at that time.

Three or four of the priests we interviewed struck us as fragile personalities with long-term ambivalences and extreme avoidance of making decisions. One told of depressions and panic attacks from adolescence on, and this convinced us that he was incapable of leading any organization or institution, let alone something as large as a Catholic parish. Another was a very dependent person who needed someone else to manage his life. We have no way to estimate the number of newly ordained priests whose personality types make them poor prospects for institutional leadership of parishes, schools, or whatever. Past research suggests that the priesthood tends to attract a number of dependent persons (Hoge et al., 1984:22). We have no doubts about these men's commitment, spirituality, and intellectual competence, but we do have doubts about their ability to lead a large organization. Probably seminarians with differing personality characteristics should be encouraged to specialize in various ministries, some of which do not require leadership.

Experiences After Ordination

For most priests, post-ordination experiences were the main factor in their feelings of satisfaction or dissatisfaction. Let us consider the case of the men who resigned. These men represent one portion of a larger group of dropouts from the total aggregation of those who began preparation for priesthood. The majority of the men who dropped out did so prior to ordination. Many seminarians, according to the accounts we heard, feel uncertainty about their vocations during seminary and, for various reasons, leave the seminary. The number who leave during seminary is greater than the number who leave the priesthood in the five years after seminary. Nobody has exact figures, but observers agree that the number is larger. Seminarians leave during seminary due to doubts about the faith, unhappiness with Church rules, hesitation about the celibacy rule, and discouragement. How about the men who leave after ordination? Why do they leave then?

We need to recall when the priests first thought seriously about leaving. For 32% in our sample, it occurred prior to ordination, and for 68%, after (see Table 2.12, 32). This indicates that about two-thirds had no serious doubts until they were in the active priesthood. What happened to these men in the few years after ordination? Did something take them unawares in their early years of priesthood? If so, what was it, and why weren't they prepared for it by their years of seminary training? If not, why had they not dropped out earlier? They had had, after all, an average of six years of seminary training. One would think that lengthy training would suffice to settle issues of faith and to fortify the student against any shocking subsequent experiences. Yet, according to the men we interviewed, this often was not the case; they were brought up short by some experiences in post-ordination priestly life.

We heard priests tell about three kinds of new experiences after ordination. First, they found themselves in a less supportive and affirming culture than heretofore. In seminary they had enjoyed a supportive, clubby, academic life. Their needs were all taken care of—their meals, their housing, their medical care, and (for most) intimacy. After ordination, things changed. Many priests found themselves in small-town parishes, living either alone or with one other priest. Some of the pastors showed no interest in spending time with them, and in a few cases the pastors rejected their company. The chancery seldom showed interest in them. Gone were the salad days when their every need was met, when faculty and family praised them and spoke of their promising futures. Now they had to fend for themselves in sometimes non-supportive environments.

Second, whereas women were not present in the seminary, in the parish they were everywhere. In the parish the young priests were working hand-in-hand with women in putting on church programs. As priests they attracted special attention from some women. Inevitably, they were attracted to certain women (even married women) with whom they were in contact, and this led to feelings, experiences, and complications for which seminary had not prepared them.

Third, a few young priests encountered disillusioning situations in parishes. In several cases the young priest found out that the pastor was using parish offerings for his own purposes or was doing dishonest bookkeeping. In other cases the pastor was discovered to be having an affair with a woman. In yet others the newly ordained priests found that the older priests were "climbers" more interested in their own career advancement than anything else. Naturally enough, upon discovering these situations, the young priests felt let down. They had not expected this, and it dampened their fervor.

Post-ordination experiences varied, and not all were negative, of course. For the majority of priests, their first years were positive, and the experiences contributed energy and zeal to the young priests' lives. Here are several examples of both kinds, positive and negative.

Positive Experiences

A diocesan priest:

> My greatest satisfaction since ordination has been being touched by people who have just shown an incredible level of holiness. Their relationship with the Lord—I pray that mine will be like that someday. The goodness of the people that I minister to, many of them, it's very touching. Also, add to that, those people whose relationship with the Church in the past wasn't what they wanted it to be—working with them and seeing a positive change. Knowing that at the end of a day, with God's help I've made a difference in someone's life. When they tell you that, I say, "Thank you, Lord, this is an honor and a privilege." It really is.

Another diocesan priest:

> I love it. I'm really bummed out that there's only twenty-four hours in a day, seven days a week. As a priest, I've got to be human. A good priest friend of mine said to me, "You've got to eat your spoonful of manure every day, and the people have got to see you eat it before they'll believe you." And he's right. They don't want me to have polished nails. They want to know that my life is lousy like their life is. They've got to know that our heat goes out in the rectory. They've got to know that I get flat tires, that I have bad breath. I can't live in an ivory palace. I've got to be real, and then my message will be real. . . . I think the greatest personal satisfaction is learning to love the people. Really love them. And bringing people to the Eucharist and the sacraments. Christ says that we're a body, and when one member suffers we all suffer. It's true.

A diocesan priest ordained five years:

> It was my last two and a half to three years when I really started to make a lot of good friends here and really get to know people and their families. So that's a great blessing. Just the sheer numbers of people that you meet. I

can't think of any other occupation where you have that much contact with that many people on a regular basis and are able to be a part of their lives in so many different ways.

A religious priest told of his work in campus ministry:

Probably one of my greatest satisfactions was going to _____ University in campus ministry. My provincial told me that they needed younger priests in that apostolate. That was just a great three years. I felt the Lord had called me to the right place, even though I did not want to leave parish ministry at first. As far as ever being discouraged, nothing really comes to mind. Well, my own sinfulness does come to mind.

Negative Experiences

A diocesan priest:

My pastor here, for years he has been an alcoholic, and nobody has had the strength to confront him. He is, in the present, in an inappropriate relationship with the business manager, who goes down to his cabin three to four times a week to take care of him. I don't think it's sexual, but I think it's like a mother coddling her child. He's a chain smoker, and the whole house, which is where the offices are, is reeking with smoke. She [the business manager] is in the house seven days a week, three hours a day, to sit with him. They will sit out on the porch or in the dining room. I saw that he would be bringing booze bottles in. You know those little airplane bottles, cordials—he had a whole drawer full of them in his room. He would open his door and this huge gush of alcohol smell would come out. Based on my history and what had gone on up to that point, this was not something that I could handle.

A resigned diocesan priest:

I had a really bad parish experience my first time. I was stationed with Irish guys. Here I was, freshly ordained. These guys played two against one, and it got so bad that I talked to Personnel after four months. I said, "This is crazy. I want out of this parish. Give me a new assignment." Then I took a vacation, went away for a couple of weeks, and met with the pastor. It so happened that he was leaving the parish. So then it was just me and the other associate—a more level playing field. It wasn't two against one any more. After that it was okay. Then he was made pastor and another Irish guy came in. It was just, "Here is your Mass schedule. Stay out of the way." There wasn't any mentoring, there wasn't a lot of management, there wasn't any inclusion. I really felt like I was the fifth wheel.

A resigned diocesan priest told of his disappointment with rectory living:

I felt like I was going to have the same experience at the rectory that I had had at the seminary. The pastor and the other associate, when they weren't saying Mass or at a committee meeting or hearing confessions or doing a marriage prep, they were in the living room watching TV. They were there for breakfast, lunch, and dinner. And that's just the way they were. And even sometimes on their day off they were there. And I thought, "That's not for me. I'm not going to be here three meals a day, seven days a week, every time I don't have something else to do." Subconsciously I knew that that was going to be kind of a tension. It didn't present itself at first, but as time went on I could see that the other associate wondered why I wasn't there as much. And then the pastor wondered why I wasn't there much. It became a little bit of a conflict with my pastor over my lack of time being spent there.

A young diocesan priest who felt insecure about his leadership abilities told of the difficulties when he arrived at his first parish. It was a large parish with a professional lay staff of seven, and just as he arrived the pastor left:

The worst part was, I was the age of their children, which was the biggest strike against me from the get-go. At the beginning they were really upset and didn't think that I could do anything or I could handle it, but then I started kind of working with the mentor pastor, Father _____. And Father _____, the head of priest personnel, came out a couple of times and he actually had to talk to the staff regarding what my role was, that I was kind of the temporary pastor of the parish, and until we kind of got them sort of straightened out, those first couple of months were rather difficult. And actually I didn't even have an official title until the first of November, and I think the only reason they gave me the official title of parochial administrator or interim pastor, whatever it was, was so that people could feel that I did have some pastoral leadership there. Otherwise they were trying to take it over as best they could.

A resigned priest told of his disillusionment with the conservative leadership from Rome:

I was thinking about everything, my experience in the priesthood, my experience in seminary, my experience of this neo-conservative, restorationist movement of these past twenty years, and how that was so at odds with the Vatican II theology of my earlier formation. I could see how this diocese of mine was going nowhere, that it was incredibly clerical, that people were hurting and that very few people were being truly cared for. And I had to acknowledge the truth, finally, that although I had my gifts, the gifts of my vocation validated many times over by the faithful, and I truly believed in it myself, I had to conclude I was not good for the priesthood at this time. I was thirty-five at the time, and I said to myself, "Edgar, if you have health for thirty-five more years of priestly ministry, what are they going to be like? Are you going to be implanting the gospel, or are you going to be fighting the system which is trying to restore a pre-Vatican II era of control from Rome?" And I had to conclude that I would actually be spending my energies not really serving God's people but that I was going to be forced to restoring an outdated model.

We heard numerous stories from resigned priests about feeling lonely and unappreciated. A resigned diocesan priest told of loneliness:

> I was in that one parish for four years. . . . I got involved with a woman, I think it was my second year after ordination. I know it was wrong. I think it was more a symptom of what I was going through—the loneliness. In some ways priests are almost sex symbols. There is an element of mystery: how can they be celibate? There is something sexually appealing about a priest in many women's eyes; this is what women have told. And so suddenly I was getting attention from women I hadn't had before. So I got involved with a woman sexually. A very unhealthy relationship.

Some of the interviewees were burdened by overwork. We heard this again and again. An active diocesan priest:

> Sometimes the scheduling is really tough. You have a day, you planned on doing a lot of office work and paper detail. And that day can blow up in two seconds with one phone call. Someone needs to be anointed or a funeral comes in, and it's going to take two days to prepare for that.

An active diocesan priest:

> Some demands are unrealistic, and as a priest you just have to know what's a realistic demand and what's an unrealistic one, and make your decisions based on that. And you have to know what you can do and what you can't do and learn to say no, which is always a hard thing, because kind of naturally you want to be compassionate. But then at times you've got to say no, I need more than two hours of sleep or whatever. I would say I do feel overworked because the demands are out there. If there were seventy hours in a day, I could fill them up with good ministry.

A resigned diocesan priest reflected on himself and his friends:

> This generation of priests has the difficult job of telling the laity that the priests cannot carry as much of the workload as they did in the past, since there are fewer of them. In some cases today's priests must ask parishioners to make major adjustments, such as closing down a parish or gathering for daily prayer rather than daily Mass. These difficult situations shift the proportion of support versus criticism that priests receive in a negative direction, affecting morale.

The experiences after ordination, some of which were discouraging, raise a question: How can resignations be reduced? One way is to reduce the frequency of negative experiences. This will not be easy (although possibly the seminaries could steer the new ordinands away from trouble-some parishes). Another way is to fortify the young priest prior to ordination so that new experiences or revelations are not so discomforting. This strikes us as more possible, and the priests we talked with agreed. In Chapter 6 we report a recommendation made by many priests: seminary training needs to be more realistic for actual parish life today.

Finally, let us note briefly several additional themes that came out in the interviews. One is about retreats. We heard priests talk repeatedly about the impact of retreats on their lives when they were of high school age and later. Also we heard them describe the inspiration they received from being close to older priests and nuns whom they respected. Both had lifelong effect.

Another topic may be important. The newly ordained priests made few complaints about bishops or religious superiors; on the contrary, most of their experiences with such persons were positive and supportive. Also, they had almost no complaints about laity, except for the demands that laypersons made on their time. Their relationships with laity were over-whelmingly positive and supportive. The priests' complaints about other people, when they had complaints, were mostly about other priests and about persons who had power in the diocese or community.

Chapter 6

Recommendations Made by the Priests

We asked all twenty-seven persons we talked with face-to-face what recommendations they would make to bishops and seminary rectors to improve seminary training and priestly life. The men had often thought deeply about this question and earnestly explained their ideas to us in the hope that our study would help disseminate their thoughts to the wider Catholic community. We promised to do what we could. The recommendations were somewhat disparate, and here we need to limit ourselves to the ones most often expressed.

The recommendations offered by the resigned priests and the active priests were a bit different, so we will present them in three sets: ideas proposed solely by active priests; ideas proposed solely by resignees; and ideas from both. We give a few reflections of our own in closing.

Recommendations Proposed Solely by Active Priests

Two ideas came solely from active priests. First, several men said they wished they had had more practical, hands-on training during seminary. An example:

> The things that priests do on a daily, weekly, monthly, yearly basis, I mean things that are important like confessions, saying Mass, baptisms, funerals, weddings, all the sacramental stuff—classes on those things ought to be requirements in the seminary program. I never practiced a wedding. I never practiced a funeral. I never did a baptism in my whole seminary experience. Yes, there were elective classes; I didn't take them. Some of my classmates took those electives, but I was taking other things. When I got in the field

and the first funeral I had to do, I'd never opened the funeral book. I'd never looked at it ever.

Other things. What are good penances? I had to learn that in the field. I felt stupid the first time I heard confessions, because I'm holding the book in my hand so I make sure I remember the prayer of absolution, and I feel like some old Irish priest, telling the person to go say three Hail Marys and an Our Father, because I didn't know what else to say.

He later added that he wished he had learned more about saints, because he had parishioners with special devotions to particular saints that seemed extreme to him, and he didn't know what to say. Other priests said they needed help on parish administration, financial management, tax preparation, even practical guides on counting the money and controlling the checkbook.

The second recommendation was the development of stronger prayer life during seminary. An example:

The development of the personal prayer life is of the essence. Now, when you get busy, what's the first thing that seems to go? It's prayer. It happens in my life too. It just kind of slips away. So the continual reinforcement and a variety of different prayers, and pastoral theology and a pastoral identity, they are key.

Another priest:

Spiritual formation is critical, because as a priest once said to me, "If you don't pray you're dead." And it's true. The moment that the prayer life goes, the moment that the breviary starts to collect dust, that's a death signal.

Ideas Proposed Solely by Resigned Priests

Two ideas were voiced solely by resigned priests. The first was mentioned by nearly all of them, so it can be seen as a near unanimous recommendation: Allow married men to serve as priests. We can understand this consensus when we recall that it would solve the most heart-rending problem experienced by the resigned priests: how to combine priesthood with love and intimacy. As one resigned priest said, "I love the priesthood and I love my wife." We might expect that the resigned priests would also favor allowing homosexual priests to live openly with male partners. This recommendation was mentioned by one or two persons, but the idea did not occur to others, so we don't know how widely it would be endorsed.

The second recommendation was to urge (or require) all seminarians to meet with psychological counselors to help explore issues from childhood that may be bothering them. One variation was to require clinical pastoral education during seminary. A resigned priest:

There are seminarians who are very afraid of looking at themselves. One of the things I would encourage is having all seminarians in counseling at some point, in dealing with basically the childhood issues. I think that some childhoods are something to survive, some of them are more joyous. I think all our childhoods affect us in ways we are very unaware of. Because of the crisis in vocations today, there is a push to get anyone who is a good guy into the priesthood, and there is not a lot of challenge. Some seminarians are wrestling with issues, often childhood issues. We need to deal with what is being wrestled with, not to push it under the carpet, not to avoid it, because it is inevitably going to come up. In my own personal opinion, when people end up leaving the priesthood or there is some misbehavior that happens, I think there are some unresolved childhood issues that are lurking. And I think many people are afraid of looking at them. I know that some seminarians are going to be afraid to look at those. And they are going to live in denial most of their lives or some of their lives. Who knows when they are going to come out?

CPE [clinical pastoral training] was a good experience for me. That was a good way of dealing with some of the issues lurking back there, and it helped surface some issues.

Another:

Make sure people are in touch with their heart. I think I made my decisions from my head. I don't think there was much about my formation in seminary, as good as it was, that truly led me to my heart. I also know for a fact that most of my mentors and spiritual directors around me didn't have the life experience or the skill to see what was happening to me. So make sure you connect people to their heart.

A religious priest in his thirties reflected on his seminary class:

I would recommend the seminary really push people about their motivations for being a priest. I was overly connected to my mom, as many priests are. Many priests are their mama's favorite boys, and they have this special connection to their mother, either because they are sensitive or because they are gay, or some combination, or they are just open. They have a very special connection to their mother, who on some level doesn't want them to get married. She wants that special connection. I know more priests whose mothers are eighty, ninety, ninety-five, and whose fathers have been dead twenty years, and their mother is their best friend, and they talk to her every Sunday night or twice a week. It's beautiful on one level and sick on another level. I lean more toward seeing the beautiful side, but I sometimes think there is a sickness here. I did have that, too, and have been healed from it, through a lot of counseling, therapy, praying, thinking, and decisions that I have made. I would suggest we explore those relationships a lot with all seminarians.

I think a lot of initial motivation for priesthood is complicated, and I didn't meet very many men in seminary who, I would say, had a balanced upbringing and normal relational life with a normal dating life. Hardly any. Most were like me. They didn't really date in college. Myself, in high school I didn't date at all really; in college I dated one woman and it was semi-normal. There is something strange about the motives why some people go into the priesthood, and it would help if they worked those out.

Recommendations Proposed by Both Resigned and Active Priests

Four recommendations were made so consistently that they represent an important groundswell. Resigned and active priests agreed on all four.

1. More openness about sexuality. Seminaries need more open discussion of sexuality in general and of topics such as celibacy and homosexuality in particular. Discussion needs to take place in classes and also in formation programs and personal counseling. One resigned priest reflected on his experience in seminary:

> We need to bring more awareness to the gay-straight question. I didn't realize there were so many gay men in my class. Though some of them were friends and even close friends, there is a different energy that happens among gay and [among] straight men and across the lines between gay and straight men.
>
> The gays I know are great priests, by and large. But in my class of ten priests, there were two straight guys out of ten. I'm not saying the other eight were totally gay, but I know for sure two of us were straight and maybe one or two others. For sure, six have either told me they are gay or told someone else. Many of them realized it when they were in seminary. How could they have a normal life experience, if you couldn't even have a normal life as a gay person in our culture? How could they come to terms with their deepest desires for relationships in that context? Very tricky. So they wrestle. One is a personal friend of mine. He wrestles a lot. He didn't know he was gay until he became ordained and fell in love with a man. He's in a sticky place now. He'll probably stay, and the reason is that he loves being with men. He's not sleeping with them, he's not genitally involved. But he's connected head or heart to these men, and that's where his energy is. He's fed. I'll be surprised if he leaves.

Another resigned priest asked for a better understanding of celibacy:

> I think guys need to be challenged more with the celibacy issue. Guys talk about it. Joke about it. Priests are guys like anybody else. Some of the young guys that are coming in have no real-life experience and should get some first. They know nothing about sex. How can a guy like this make a commitment to this life he knows nothing about? I think the seminary needs to talk openly about the relationship between celibacy and priesthood. When I was

in grade school, I remember the nuns saying to us, "You don't need to worry about if you are called to priesthood, because if you are, God would never give you the call to priesthood without giving you the call to celibacy too." What does that mean? I don't know, but that's our *modus operandi* still: we don't need to discuss it, because if you have a call to the priesthood you have a call to celibacy. And I think that the Church needs to be realistic with guys in the seminary and say, "You know what? It is perfectly all right for you to feel absolutely called to the priesthood and not feel called to celibacy. There's nothing wrong with that. It's absolutely fine. We're not going to let you be a priest, but it's absolutely fine. There's no problem with that." Be that clear. Now we have the presumption that you are called to the priesthood and also want to live celibately. Nobody ever talks about, "Do you really want to live celibately? What does it mean?"

There's a lot of talk at the spiritual level about intimacy, intimacy with other people. It's not wrong. It's absolutely correct. You have to have that intimacy with God and intimacy with other people. But marriage and intimacy with a single person is totally different from any of that. With all due respect, the guys that are doing the talking about it have no idea.

There is a lot of emotional garbage when you really get intimate with a person and have to deal with that person. As a priest you can avoid that so easily. You can have all the intimacy you want on your terms without having to deal with your own stuff.

A resigned priest:

Sexuality was a completely taboo word [in seminary], from my spiritual director to my faculty advisor to whoever else would choose to use it. The only time the discussion about sexuality came up was in the classroom, where it was a very academic discussion. And then it was defending yourself, your own personal experience, academically. And while that was challenging and kind of engaging, it didn't help me personally. It was very intellectual. So I didn't feel I grew as a person, and I didn't feel a lot of support to grow as a person in these areas.

Another resigned priest:

We need more frank discussion in seminary. I can remember the student master giving his weekly chapter talks, and they covered everything, including chastity and temptations against chastity, and I don't know how it could have been handled better, but it needs to be handled better as far as homosexuality is concerned. Just like stating, "Of the persons in this room, there's a certain percentage of you who are [homosexual] and some who are very experienced. It's higher than in the general population. That's not a bad or judgmental thing; it's just a statement of fact. You are going to be perceived this way, whether you are or not. How are you going to handle it?"

Maybe have a young priest come in who is homosexually oriented and say, "This is part of who I am. This is part of what I struggle with. These are the temptations against chastity that I have." Fine. Have someone come in who's a heterosexual priest to tell his feelings. "This is what happens when a married woman comes in, or a sixteen-year-old girl. These are the type of things that have happened to me." What we had seemed too abstract. And we needed the same type of talk about alcoholism. Be more concrete.

Active priests had similar suggestions:

The whole homosexuality thing, the seminaries need to get over their fear of that. I mean, not that it should be encouraged, but they've got to talk to the guys. It's got to be dealt with. If you're going to train and ordain men to a celibate priesthood, you've got to talk about all the aspects of sexuality and how that relates to living celibately. My feeling was, if a guy would have brought a girl into the seminary and it got out that these two were having sex in the seminary, he would have been kicked out in a heartbeat. But there were dozens of stories of two guys sleeping together, and nobody ever got kicked out of the seminary. And no one's talking about it. It's all the gossip and whispering in the house. "Does the faculty know about this? Are they going to do anything?"

An active priest:

I know a lot of gay priests. And they're good men. They're holy men. I don't judge them. I listen to their stories as a man and fellow minister. I know exactly what they're going through. I challenge them: "I don't care if you are gay or straight or whatever, just be men of integrity. Yes, we are called to a life of celibacy, and I know priests who are also in straight relationships. If that relationship causes you to be a more loving and compassionate priest, I don't have a problem with that. I don't. Be loving. Just don't be an S-O-B to the people of God. We all need to be loved and to feel love."

An active priest now serving as an assistant director of formation in a seminary:

The sexual orientation issue is one issue that we need to look at more carefully. . . . What I find is that whether in a diocese or a religious order, people at the top are not comfortable going into that conversation. I don't blame them, because we are all uncomfortable to a certain degree. We are all very vulnerable, and I would not want to force anyone out of the closet. If the environment of religious life is not allowing someone to feel comfortable enough to be free to talk about who they are, this needs to change.

2. More realistic seminary training. Provide more real-life experiences during seminary training, including having a pastoral year away and having women in some seminary classes. A resigned priest:

If there were a way to afford people in training more opportunities to be in roles that are similar to the ones they will be in when they're priests, it might help people kind of prepare for that role or make decisions about assuming it a little earlier. In some ways I wish that I had been forced to go into parishes and preach and be a part of it. And have all those projections from the congregation onto me in this role, so that I would have had to struggle with them earlier.

Another resigned priest:

Experience in a seminary can be very different than the experience in a parish. That is, a lot of my affective needs were met in a seminary, especially in our seminary, which was related to a university, where you are meeting lots of people and engaged in lots of different things. There were women my age in my classes that were friends, that met some of my affective needs for relationships with women. Then I get into a parish that is mostly elderly people and a few younger people, and those needs weren't met. The experience was very different for me. In seminary I think I could have done celibacy for another decade. But in the parish, I was dying on the vine. We must help guys have an experience somehow, somewhere, of real parish life for a couple of years where they are working in a parish, if that's at all possible.

One resigned priest praised his seminary for having other people in the classes:

I thought it was great to be in classes with women and men getting their master's in theology, also with permanent deacons who were taking classes. We had a wide spectrum and variety of different people. As a matter of fact, we were actually outnumbered about two to one by lay students. I didn't think it hurt my priestly identity at all to study with lay men and women. After all, they'd be the people I'd be working with and ministering with, and in the parish I'd be the minority on staff. The majority would be lay ministers, men and women, so I thought it was only natural. To take a class on marriage with married lay people, I think it made a lot of sense, because they had some wonderful insights. And to take classes on family issues and counseling, it made a lot of sense to me that they should be there.

Another resigned priest:

We need to alter the seminary environment so it is less amenable to becoming a truly all-encompassing and secure home and more of a foretaste of what a priest's life will be. Once I entered the seminary, I had a built-in, institutional support system for daily living as well as interpersonally; my living environment included dozens of interesting peers, kind parental figures, three meals a day, and economic security. This living situation is unlike what life is like as a priest today. The priest often lives alone and, while certain parishioners become true friends, most of his contact is with "consumers" of his professional services. He is wholly responsible for designing and carving out the kind of interpersonal and daily living support he needs. This is so even if the priest shares the rectory with others. Based on my observations, it is rare that a priest happens to be assigned with another priest or group of priests who can fill the role of a compatible, close, emotionally supportive friend.

3. Give more attention to the newly-ordained. Bishops and chancery officers should give more attention to new priests, and older priests serving as mentors should be more available to help them. A resigned priest:

> Now there is a wall between the chancery and the priests. I don't even know if they know what goes on in suburban parishes. I'm sure the bishop and chancery staff are busy. But never once in my first four years did a bishop call me up and say "I want to meet with you for fifteen minutes just to see how you are doing." There was no contact. It was all crisis management. Their attitude was, "We have a problem here, and we are going to put it out. But if you're not a problem, then everything must be fine." Now in my job at the office, I talk to my boss weekly. I tell him what's going on. He is involved. He asks what he can do to help me. The bishops need to take a lesson from the business world. Why don't we have happy priests? There is no contact. And you wonder why guys are leaving.

A resigned priest:

> The newly ordained in my diocese, there were just two of us, we had a once-a-quarter get-together with a priest who was part of the priest personnel board. We would have an overnight where we'd kind of share and talk about what it is like our first year. It was good, but it just wasn't enough. There wasn't enough there. It was more like a retreat than a chance to really talk about what's going on in the parish. I think a more formal mentoring program would have been better. And maybe being assigned a specific mentor from one of the experienced priests in the diocese.

An active priest:

> Bishop _____ does a very good thing. He gets together with the guys six months after ordination for a six-month checkup. He'll call them and bring them in to talk about how things are going. I know for a number of guys it's been a very positive thing. They've had an opportunity to talk very honestly to him about the way things are.
>
> Personnel boards should also follow up with the guys and ask how things are going. Show them that we haven't forgotten about you; you're very important. They need to value the input from the young guys, encouraging them to participate in diocesan structures and organizations. I'm only four years ordained, but I was talking with the director of the personnel board, and he was very supportive. He said, "I think that this is a good thing to hear from you. The board needs representation that's truly representative of every age

group. Having young guys represented makes them feel like you are important, you are needed, and we need your input."

I also think the seminary should invite guys back for liturgy, just a simple thing like that. Invite them back to talk to guys who are in third and fourth theology about their experiences, maybe talk to the guys who are going to be ordained.

Another active priest:

Bishops should meet with their young priests every six months. They should meet with them as a group and then pull them out individually just for twenty minutes. And in that twenty minutes he should know who their spiritual directors are, how often they're going to confession, and are they having any struggles. They need to know that they're supported. It's awfully hard for an outfielder to stand in the sun and keep shagging flies, hour after hour, day after day, unless the coach runs out every once in a while with a Coke and says, "You're doing a great job, keep it up." A lot of these priests feel isolated in their positions out there. They've got nobody.

4. More support programs. Encourage support programs and gatherings of priests where they can share their experiences. A number of priests suggested support groups that discuss real issues, not just exchange courtesies. A resigned priest:

I recommend some sort of support group, facilitated by an outsider, where issues are dealt with, such as celibacy, preaching, relationships, friendships, intimacy, and workload. A support group specifically of newly ordained, facilitated by either a counselor or a priest who is very astute in being able to help people in these situations.

A resigned priest talked about support he never got from other priests:

After I left seminary, I felt a great loss in many ways. I lost a lot of my really good friends who were sent far away. I feel like the minute my foot left the seminary door, I lost all that camaraderie. I had no good mentoring, and I rarely got together with my classmates. It was too hard. No one got me involved in a priest support group, which I wish they would have. I would have been open to it, but I never got asked. I just felt like, besides some occasional cocktail hours, I didn't get together with other priests too often. It was like the minute you got out there, everyone was too wrapped up and busy, and then when they were free, they didn't want to spend time with priests or more ministry people. They didn't want to do church stuff.

They should encourage relationships between priests as much as possible. Stress the importance of district meetings and convener meetings and all of that to being healthy, and that it is not taking time away from your parish assignment or the people. You can't be guilty for doing those things. This is part of ministry and part of the priesthood.

Reflections on the Research

Allow me a few reflections on this project. For the past two and a half years, our research team has labored to produce reliable information on the first five years of priesthood. We knew that the research would touch on prickly questions about the priesthood today, and therefore we have been cautious at every step. Viewpoints of priests are very disparate, and any new research finding is bound to be rejected by one faction or another. In light of this, our purpose has been to produce information as trustworthy and as free from partisan bias as possible.

We leave to commentators the task of spelling out practical implications of our findings. Here I will merely reflect briefly on the project.

We found evidence of change over time. Andrew Greeley made an excellent study of resignations and priestly morale in 1970, and it serves as a good benchmark for viewing conditions thirty years later. We found that the reasons some priests were demoralized and thinking about resigning were a bit different in 2000 than they had been in 1970. In 1970, the main two reasons for resignation were the desire to marry and a rejection of authoritative institutional Church structures. In 2000 the desire to marry was clearly in first place, with institutional criticism far behind. The priests in our 2000 research were not, for the most part, institutional rebels. It is true they came disproportionately from the liberal wing of the priesthood, but they seldom espoused serious institutional reforms. The most common institutional reform the priests espoused was optional celibacy for priests. Why were there fewer calls for reform in 2000? We do not know. Maybe because the priests liked the existing system or maybe because they saw little possibility of anything happening. Maybe a different type of man is entering the priesthood.

Our study was suffused with talk about celibacy, loneliness, desire for intimacy, and homosexuality—more so than we expected. Much of this is not new, but the frank talk about homosexuality is something new. Either past researchers did not find the same level of concern, or they hesitated to report what they heard. My guess is that the situation today is new. Today in the United States homosexuality is being discussed more openly than ever in the past. This is true in government, business, and religion. Nobody, then, should be surprised if new research on priests finds more openness about homosexuality than there was earlier. It is happening everywhere. Whereas in the past many priests and seminary faculty found homosexuality too embarrassing to talk about, today that reticence has subsided, and people more readily voice their feelings. We have reported many feelings in this book. It is a fair bet that aversive feelings about homosexuality will continue to cool down in coming years in society overall and also in the priesthood. What was taboo to talk about in the past will be less taboo in the future. This whole question cries out for more openness and more research.

The issue of priestly overwork also needs more examination. We lacked information to do it here, but someone needs to clarify if (a) the new priests are actually working harder than their counterparts did in the past, or (b) their attitudes toward work are different. And if, as I believe, the demands on newly ordained priests have intensified, someone needs to consider what changes in definitions and expectations are needed in parish life. I am convinced that we cannot continue the received traditions about priestly obligations ("But the pastor always took care of _____").

In the end, what can be done about morale and resignations? A lot needs to be done. Life is one adjustment after another, and this is as true for institutions as it is for individuals. Let me try to distinguish two types of adjustments: easy ones and difficult ones. Several easy adjustments were recommended by the priests and reported in this chapter. They have to do with improving living conditions, managing problems of overwork and burnout, and making seminary programs more practical. Difficult adjustments, more formidable to envision and realize, will very likely be needed later in face of the worsening priest shortage. Possibly the number of priests could be increased by offering optional celibacy under certain conditions, upgrading the diaconate, or making some ecumenical arrangement. If that is not done, priests will need to adjust to future parish life in which priests are spread thin and lay ministers carry out most of the leadership. The option of simply saying no to all these possibilities does not exist; trends are moving too quickly to maintain the conditions now in place.

The present research has said little about the larger problem of the dwindling supply of priests. We leave that to others. Our point here is simply that while we have discussed small adjustments to priestly life in this book, they will probably not be enough in the long run. A large agenda lies ahead.

The New Context for Priestly Ministry

Rev. George E. Crespin

The study of *The First Five Years of the Priesthood* does not reveal any significantly new information. It does point out, however, that the context in which these new priests are living out their ministerial lives is different from the past and continues to change.

What is this new context? The study describes it well. First, there are fewer priests than in the past and not a lot of reason to believe that this will change dramatically in the near future. Second, there are more Catholics than ever, and the makeup of the Catholic population in this country is more complex than ever. The net result is that there is more work to be done, and the diversity of the Catholic population creates new opportunities as well as challenges for a priestly ministry. Third, there is a whole different attitude toward authority. Today, authority and respect are qualities that have to be earned rather than automatically given. Fourth, we are living in a time of changing sexual mores, and these affect both the people who are served by the clergy as well as the attitudes of the clergy themselves. The study mentions several times the tension that exists between the so-called "straight" clergy and the "gay" clergy. Fifth, there are clearly different ecclesiologies at work, and this is an additional source of tension within the clergy itself.

Finally, there is one issue that does not get much attention in the study. It is one that I feel certainly is a source of concern in the area where I minister as a pastor: the additional pressure on priests who are bilingual and bicultural. With so many different cultures and languages present in the church on the West Coast, and I suspect in other parts of the country as well, those priests who are able to relate to more than one culture are in effect expected to do double duty. Not only are they expected to attend to the needs of the people from whose culture they come, but they are also expected to tend to the needs of the rest of the Catholic population in their care. This presents a new challenge and could become a potential problem.

These new cultural and theological contexts as well as the findings of this study call for a number of actions that are crucial for the success of new priests, and for that matter, for any clergy.

Because of these more complex and often conflicting demands, new clergy need to possess a higher level of maturity than was necessary in previous times. The role of the priest has not only changed, but he is frequently under question or attack. Because of this, the new priest has to have a clear sense of who he is and what he is about in order to be able to function adequately as well as to survive.

Today's reality also calls for a deeper level of psychological integration for the priest to be able to minister effectively. He needs to be in touch with his own needs and limitations and also be integrated with himself as a sexual person. The "wounded healer" may be an apt description of the priestly minister, but it is more imperative than ever that he be in touch with his woundedness and able to grapple with it in a constructive way.

The new priest has to be a man of deep faith, with a sense and vision of the Gospel mission. The challenge includes providing the Eucharist for all the Church's members. It also includes providing pastoral leadership in an effective, consistent way to assure that future generations will be able to experience the tradition and the culture of the Church.

In the face of the challenges described above, this is what I believe the study calls for in terms of seminary formation and the time immediately thereafter.

A prayer life and relational skills

Both priests who have stayed and those who have left assert the need for a solid prayer life based on strong faith in Jesus' mission for the Church. The research also indicates a clear need for the development of relational skills on the part of the candidates. Priests today deal with a variety of men and women in the context of ministry in a parish on a day-to-day basis—pastoral administrators, pastoral assistants, pastoral council leaders, to name a few. This interaction calls for the need to deal with them effectively in all circumstances without feeling threatened or losing a sense of self.

Sexuality and sexual issues, including orientation

Having been ordained at a time when issues about sexuality were never discussed, except in the context of celibacy, it had been my hope that the gift of sexuality would have been addressed more forthrightly and openly. The study seems to indicate otherwise. An open, honest, and frank discussion about sexuality is needed either in small or large groups. It is a delicate issue, but the fact that it needs to be done seems obvious to me, both in diocesan and religious order seminaries.

The importance of the new priest's first assignment

Having been on our diocesan Priest Placement Board for over twenty years, I find that the common wisdom has always been that the first assignment of a new priest was crucial in terms of preparing the way for his future ministry. It was also an important factor in determining whether the new priest would survive past his first five years in his ministerial life. The study clearly indicates the critical need to focus energy on the importance of this transitional time. Because of the dwindling number of priests, the temptation might be to short-circuit this process. But for that very reason it is more important than ever for the new priest to be assigned to a pastor who has a strong and inspiring pastoral vision. This means that the first assignment cannot be with just any pastor, but with one who is patient yet not overbearing or overly directive. It might be difficult to find this combination of gifts and talents in the first-assignment pastor, but not taking the time and effort to make this match could prove to be a serious mistake.

The importance of mentoring

Closely allied to the importance of the first assignment is the value of the assignment of a mentor for the newly ordained. I find lip service given to the value and need of a mentor. The study indicates the value of this practice. Yet, my experience indicates that the assignment of a mentor often does not take place, and if it does, it is only mildly effective. I am not aware of a program, at least in our area of the country, where there is such a practice of mentors for newly ordained priests. There is a strong insistence on the new priest having a spiritual director/confessor, but to my knowledge there is no widespread practice of mentoring. Like the newly ordained's first pastor, the mentor has a specific role to play in the initiation of the newly ordained. He should be detached, objective, and not an authority figure. He must be someone with whom the newly ordained can be comfortable.

A personal relationship with the bishop

The final point in the formation and transition process is the bishop's personal relationship with the newly ordained. According to the study, the absence of this relationship can give a sense that the new priest is just another cog in the wheel of an unwieldy diocese. Because of the size of a diocese and other episcopal commitments, this relationship may take different forms. The point is that this is the third and probably most important part of the transition process for the newly ordained. The study indicates through their personal stories that both priests who have stayed and those who have left ministry value the connectedness to the bishop and, through him, the rest of the diocese. Bishops may wish to note that the stakes seem rather high: establishing a relationship with the newly ordained should be a priority.

A *member of the presbyterate*

I think it is important for the new man to feel connected to the diocese beyond the parish to which he is assigned.

1) An effort should to made to introduce the newly ordained to diocesan and presbyteral structures. This would include the presbyteral council or its various committees and task forces.

2) In the early years diocesan personnel should pay attention to attendance of the new priest at clergy formation programs and events. My experience is that patterns are set early on in a new priest's experience and that often, for whatever reason, he does not feel a part of such opportunities. My observation is that those in charge of such events do not adequately question the young priest as to why he is absenting himself from these opportunities, both to develop his ministerial skills as well as to become part of the presbyterate. Comments are often made that "Father Bob Jones never attends any of our gatherings," but does anyone ever ask why?

3) I did not see any mention of ongoing education as a factor in the experience of the new priest. It is my experience and conviction that we need to seriously look at how we are going to continue to develop and motivate our new priests. We cannot use the excuse of a shortage to reduce or postpone the new priest's opportunity for further study. This mentality strikes me as tremendously shortsighted, because we need both to encourage these men and better prepare them for the very uncertain future they face. I have seen firsthand what a negative response to this kind of desire has produced. Rather than discourage the newly ordained, they need to be affirmed in their desire to broaden their ministerial skills and academic ability.

Priests' support groups

One of the most important options for the newly ordained priest is participation in a priests' support group. It is my conviction that not participating in this activity is missed opportunity. There are very few settings for serious and confidential discussion to take place about the challenges of being an effective priestly minister on a day-to-day basis. A support group provides this context and is a source of encouragement and spiritual sustenance to any priest. I doubt whether mandatory participation in a support group would be helpful. Suffice it to say that in my experience, sharing the paschal mystery through a priests' support group can be a source of healing, compassion, prayer, and intimacy.

Priestly accountability

For all practical purposes, priests are accountable to no one if they so choose, whether in the area of their personal lives or their pastoral ministry. The unstated mentality is that a priest is a grown mature man who has been properly prepared for his position and therefore is not subject to a system of accountability. Only if a priest is seriously involved in some kind of questionable or scandalous activity is he called to account. The Second Vatican Council introduced some structures of accountability in the ongoing life of the Church (e.g., finance committees at the diocesan and parish levels) but largely skipped ordained ministry.

By accountability I do not mean the heavy-handed, authoritarian style that existed in some dioceses in previous generations. That was fear, not accountability. What I am suggesting is that there needs to be a wide discussion in the dioceses and among the clergy about how we can be more accountable for our pastoral life and practices, both to those in authority as well as to our coworkers in ministry. Accountability can best be exercised through the practice of spiritual direction. Other structures of pastoral evaluation and accountability need to either be put in place or more effectively implemented. My concern is that even though in the seminary there may have been structures of evaluation, both by faculty and by peers, when a young man is sent into ministry as an ordained priest, few if any of those structures or systems are present. When they are present, at least in theory, they often do not operate in practice.

Timing of the first pastorate

There is the growing practice of giving the recently ordained major responsibilities for parishes. I realize that the shortage of priests is the main reason why these men are being made pastors sooner than they would have been in previous generations. But the impact of this needs to be weighed carefully, and some safeguards need to be put in place to avoid any unnecessary stresses and tensions in the lives of recently ordained priests. This is one more reason why the newly ordained's first assignment is so important.

At the beginning of this commentary I stated that *The First Five Years of the Priesthood* does not reveal any significantly new information, but what has changed is the context in which the newly ordained priests live their ministerial lives. Seminary formation is key to the development of the spiritually, psychologically, and physically healthy priest. It is more important than ever in an increasingly diverse and changing priesthood.

Reverend Crespin is pastor of St. Joseph the Worker Parish in Berkeley, California. He has served as chancellor, vicar for priests, and nearly twenty years as a member of the Priest Placement Board of the Oakland diocese.

Church and Challenge for the Newly Ordained

Most Rev. Thomas J. Curry

I found this to be an excellent study—comprehensive, varied, and thorough. Its mixture of survey reporting/analysis and personal interviews is both interest-sustaining and enlightening as to the situation of newly ordained priests in the Church today.

My response does not provide a critique of the study, because I do not have one. Neither does it proceed from an analysis of how to apply the data it has provided. Rather, I have chosen to use the study as a launching point for a brief reflection on what it tells us about the condition of the Church generally and of the newly ordained priests particularly at this juncture in history. My comments are in no way meant to be critical of those who conducted the study. On the contrary, I feel that in helping exemplify the circumstances the Church finds itself in today and promoting an examination of that situation, they have made a most significant contribution.

The overall impression I took away from the study was that the newly ordained priests are in the main cultivating their own gardens, with a good deal of contentment but without much knowledge of, or concern for, how they connect with the larger Church, and that they view other priests as generally doing the same. What struck me most strongly about the survey, as regards both its conceptualization and the responses to it, was the lack of a strong sense of vision, of an understanding of the urgency of the dilemma now facing the Church, of a passion derived from such an understanding, or of an awareness of the importance of finding a new way to evangelize and catechize.

The survey deals comprehensively and well with why priests leave; however, it is far less enlightening as to why they stay or should stay. With regard to the latter, the strongest impression I derive from the data is that priests stay because the Church is meeting their needs. If this is the case, it gives rise to the question of whether the individualism that is so prevalent in our society has not overwhelmed the Church, too, whether we are conforming to society rather than attempting to transform it. My point is certainly not to argue that priests' needs should not be met, but rather to ask how those needs can be met in a way that is most fulfilling for the priests and effective for the people of God.

Whereas I see a great discontinuity between the Church of today and, for example, that of the 1970s, the survey appears to me to show hardly any discontinuity. My own ministerial situation will serve to illustrate this point. Based on ethnic calculations, the Archdiocese of Los Angeles has a possible Catholic population of five million people. The parishes report that they serve about two million people. Let me hasten to add that to me this discrepancy does not reflect failure on the part of priests or their parishes. The Church here is vibrant. Parishes have made enormous strides in their efforts to accommodate the influx of immigrants.

What we face today is a major challenge that is structural as well as a ministerial. Since the later 1940s, parishes have been formed to accommodate the shift in population from cities to suburbs and the internal migration from the East and Midwest to the West and Southwest. Many of these parishes were built to accommodate what were then regarded as great numbers of people, e.g., 1500–2000 families. Now, however, many of those same parishes find themselves ministering to 3000–4000 families, although census projections have indicated there may be 10,000 or more possibly Catholic households within their boundaries.

Perhaps never in the history of the Church have parishes served so many people so well. However, our life as a Church is overwhelmingly caught up in responding to daily challenges, solving immediate problems, completing tasks that cannot be put off. We do not really have a plan—are not even conscious of the need for a plan—for reaching out to those "possibly Catholic households" in our midst. We are boxed in by the reality of parishes structured to meet the needs of the Church as it existed before the present immigration. We often identify evangelization as asking people to come home, to come back to church. But what passion can priests have for such a mission, inundated as they are by the huge populations they are currently serving?

The last thirty years have seen the greatest concentrated influx of immigrants, many of them Catholic, in American history. We are living in a time comparable to that of the generation before World War I (although the percentage of foreign-born to native-born was higher then), when the country experienced a period of enormous immigration and the Church had to adjust to immense numbers of non-English-speaking Catholics from abroad.

We are living in a time of urgency: a window of opportunity to embrace, serve, and evangelize the immigrants exists, but it will not remain open for long. I found no sense of such urgency in the study, however. It seems to proceed unaware of the enormous increase in the Catholic population over the past thirty years. Granted, this time the immigration is more concentrated in the West. I suspect, though, that the situation we face in Los Angeles represents that of much of the rest of the country, only more so.

We are often reminded that inactive Catholics constitute perhaps the largest religious category in the country. Although the study notes some of the changes resulting from Vatican II, as well as others proceeding from societal developments, neither in its fundamental assumptions nor in the responses of the priests is there any consciousness of the enormous changes and challenges that have come from the immigration of the past thirty years. Not only do we have more people and fewer priests, as the study indicates, but many of our parishes have been flooded with non-English-speaking newcomers, bringing with them different cultures and completely different experiences of the Church.

How is the Church to cope with this phenomenon? How are we to evangelize and catechize this tremendous new population? Are the newly ordained even aware of that challenge? I could not determine from the study whether they know it lies before them, much less have any concept of its dimensions. Yet it is a challenge that confronts us all, and that is most crucial for them, because they have more years to serve.

In his pastoral letter *As I Have Done for You,* Cardinal Roger Mahony wrote that "mere adjustments and shifts in practice will not suffice. What is called for is a major reorientation in our thinking about ministry as well as in ministerial practice." Integrating the laity in the mission of the Church to a greater extent than heretofore is part of this vital transformation. The study does mention empowerment, but, as in the Church at large, that concept is hardly explored. How are the laity to become real collaborators and sharers in the mission? We know that we will have more paid staff in the future, but how will such staff and other lay leaders be more than "Father's helpers?" If so, how are we to even begin to envision the changes that will bring about? And how will such changes impact the lives and the role of priests in the future? The newly ordained priests mention that they are busy and at times overwhelmed with work. However, the study seems to indicate little sense among them that what they are doing differs in any essential fashion from what priests did when there were far more of them and far fewer of the laity, and when the mission of the Church was less complex.

To some extent, the study seems to proceed from an assumption that the problems it uncovers and highlights—loneliness, the difficulty of living a celibate life, the need for connectedness with fellow priests—can be addressed head-on. However, the answer to those issues will come mostly by indirection; such solutions will be the by-products of a life lived with a sense of mission, passion, direction, and longing. It appears to equate dissatisfaction with unhappiness, but the two are not necessarily synonymous. One can have a profound sense of dissatisfaction with one's own limitations and the disparity between one's ideals and achievement and nevertheless be profoundly fulfilled in striving toward a goal.

Priests settle for the statement that differing ecclesiology divides us. The very use of this term separates us from the vast majority of Catholics, who have no idea what we are talking about. But do the priests themselves know what we mean by "differing ecclesiology"? Do they allow theological jargon to conceal what may be unexamined preferences, prejudices, and experiences? The study gives little hint as to the priests' image and sense of the Church or of their own mission as related to the Church. The desire of the "orthodox" to restore the Church supposedly destroyed after Vatican II is at least a symptom that newly ordained priests want some sense of a bigger picture. If, absent a deep and thoughtful conceptualization of the mission of the Church and a clear and inspiriting perception of their own mission within it, they continue to see the Church as simply meeting their own needs, the people they serve will approach the Church in the same fashion, leading, as the study indicates, to an exacerbation of the feeling that the priests are overwhelmed by the overwhelming demands of the people.

Enabling the newly ordained to articulate an ecclesiology, that is, to have a vision of what the Church should be for our society and of their place in that vision, seems to be the most pressing need of the Church at large. If it remains unfilled, the newly ordained will have to continue to cope, to function well (as they obviously do), but possibly be destined to lives spent reacting to needs without any sense of overall purpose, and ultimately leading them to focus on protecting themselves from the people rather than on assuming positions of leadership.

The survey tends to confirm my existing impression that at the present time, the clergy and many others in the Church have reached a plateau. Currently we are resting from wrestling with the large questions, taking care of ourselves, occupying ourselves primarily with the business at hand. Some have interrupted this lull with proclamations to the effect that the Church has been a failure, that we have to recover an imagined past. The reality, however, is that we find ourselves in a downtime, not because we have failed, but because we have been so successful. The modern Church, particularly in America, has successfully scaled so many peaks that it needed a time of rest and quiet.

In our own time, the Church has implemented a thoroughgoing revolution in ecumenical thinking and in its relationship with other religions.

What was a dominant attitude for 450 years has been completely reversed in only 20. Partly as a result of the Declaration on Religious Liberty, we have transformed our relationship with the world outside the Church. We have reoriented the whole of Catholic life to the Scriptures, something largely lost to Catholicism for ages. We have taught Catholics and many others to more profoundly appreciate the connection between religion and social teaching. We have reformed and renewed the liturgy in the most revolutionary way in history. And through all these changes, the clergy, particularly pastors, have mediated, negotiated, explained, and balanced pressure from both above and below. The now passing generation of priests and pastors shepherded the Church through its greatest transformation since the early Christians decided to preach to the Gentiles, and the Church is today more vibrant than ever.

Neither older priests nor the Church at large, however, can convey a passion to the newly ordained until we recover our sense of the Church since Vatican II. We need to hearten the coming generation of priests to meet the challenges they will encounter, to encourage them by reminders of what has been accomplished, and not allow them to be deceived by those who have no knowledge of the past.

My hope for the study is that it will not add to the multitudinous demands that have been made on our seminaries, which have generally served the Church excellently. I pray never to hear another recommendation that formation programs should train seminarians how better to balance checkbooks! Given the percentage of the Church's GNP currently devoted to seminaries and vocation programs, we do not need an increase of spending here. Continuing to expend more and more on fewer and fewer is not a wise course for the future.

I enjoy visiting the clergy and appreciate the importance of doing so. However, I long for the day when my visits can consist of more than affirming them, telling them truthfully they are doing a very good job, and then asking them if they are taking care of their spiritual life, taking time off for vacation, and getting together with other priests. That we have to ask these things, and that the survey at hand focused so much on them, is an indication that we are not currently immersed in the type of overall tasks and challenges that would provide somewhat of an antidote to the sense of loneliness and lack of connectedness that featured so prominently in the responses.

Priests are so deeply occupied in dealing with the trees that they have no time to locate a vantage point from which to see the extent and shape of the forest that surrounds them. The way to address the issues raised by this survey is to recover a sense of the magnitude of that forest and challenge them to look beyond their own immediate thickets. If we are to go forward, priests will need to recover a sense of where they have come from and perhaps a greater confidence than they currently possess of how successful they have been as pathfinders.

After the last huge immigration, Gerald Shaughnessy published a much-quoted book entitled *Has the Immigrant Kept the Faith?* (1925). Today's newly ordained priests and their successors will probably be in a position to ask a similar question in the not too distant future. To meet the challenges of the future, the Catholic community will need to wrestle with the great questions of mission, definition, evangelization, and catechesis. Reading the study, one can be generally optimistic that the newly ordained will be very willing to engage in this great exploration.

Most Reverend Curry is an auxiliary bishop of the Los Angeles archdiocese and regional bishop of the Santa Barbara region.

The Study's Implications Related to Health

Rev. James J. Gill, S.J., M.D.

Dean Hoge's illuminating study, *The First Five Years of the Priesthood,*
sheds needed light on the manifold aspects of a priest's personal life and
ministry during a crucial phase of his development. The findings reported
clearly highlight the many and often serious problems faced by men who
remain in the priesthood as well as by those who resign. Priests, seminarians, formation personnel, and Church leaders stand to benefit enormously
from Hoge's well-designed and intelligibly presented research. But the
benefits will be derived only at a cost of profound consideration of the experiences of the priests studied, followed by serious and imaginative efforts to make the changes required in priestly formation, assignments, work,
and style of life.

The comments I want to offer are related to the physical and mental
health of the priests studied and those ordained before and after them.
What struck me repeatedly during several readings of the report is how
much emotional stress and concomitant suffering these lives revealed. A
wide variety of distressful emotions can easily be recognized as underlying
a great number of the replies tabulated and discussed in the first half of the
report. In the latter chapters, the interviews, so well accomplished by the
researchers, elicited countless explicit expressions of painful aspects of
these priests' affective lives.

No ordained minister I've known has told me that he was experiencing a
pain-free existence. A priest's life and work are fraught with a variety of
inevitable difficulties. But what emerged from the study, as I read it, is
alarming evidence of the too numerous ways in which stress that is pre-
ventable is being encountered by priests today. When there is considerable
stress in a priest's life, especially if the experience is chronic, physicians

recognize it as a natural threat to the health of his body or mind. Harm to relationships, ministry, and spiritual life are also likely to ensue.

Look at a few examples of the frequently reported stresses the study includes; they all involve an obvious frustration of the needs or desires a significant number of priests brought with them into their earliest post-ordination assignments:

- chronic loneliness

- feeling overwhelmed with work

- lack of privacy

- difficulty living a celibate life

- non-involvement in decision-making and pastoral planning

- unrealistic demands and expectations of lay people

- lack of leisure time

- inadequate living quarters

- lack of expressed appreciation

- heavy-handed treatment by Church authorities

- not enough support from fellow priests

- tension in representing some of the Church's official teachings

- disagreements over ecclesiology and ministry

A word about the needs and desires so many priests find unfulfilled. The way I am using the terms here, needs are necessities—if not fulfilled, some form of personal harm is experienced. (Think of the connection between our need for food and starvation, or our need to feel esteemed and depression.) What we desire is what we want, but if we do not get it, we will be disappointed but not inevitably damaged. (Consider desiring a room with a lovelier view or apple pie for dessert tonight.) It is important to keep in mind that there are some things that one group of people only desire while others truly need them. Examples would be marriage or employment.

The study reveals that the desires and needs of many priests are not being adequately fulfilled. And whenever specific desires or needs are not being met, the God-designed automatic result is a sense of frustration accompanied usually by anger. The anger may be consciously experienced, or it may be repressed and kept unrecognized. But often the anger is spontaneously converted into the emotion we call hostility; someone is blamed for the deprivation and is dealt with antagonistically. At other times the anger is transformed into emotional depression, and blame for dissatisfaction is directed toward the self, with a resultant lowering of a person's self-esteem.

These feelings are all to some degree painful to experience. They prompt us to look elsewhere for the fulfillment of what we believe we need or to seek an effective way, if possible, to satisfy our desire. The problem is, while the frustration goes on being experienced, the body is going through a "fight or flight" reaction physiologically. If the experience of this dissonance operates intensely over a period of time, it could result in physical illness, medical researchers Walter Cannon and Hans Selye state.

Hoge's study did not intend to explore the types and degrees of illness I'm sure many of his frustrated priests were experiencing. However, it is important for us priests to keep in mind the fact that research has abundantly demonstrated that heart disease, high blood pressure, arthritis, chronic fatigue, colitis, insomnia, migraine headaches, alcoholism, other forms of addiction, diabetes, and many additional disorders are caused or exacerbated by the emotions mentioned above and many affective states related to them, such a loneliness, disillusionment, and resentment.

Priests with deep-seated needs or desires that are unmet, with resulting painful emotions, are obviously going to find it difficult to enjoy the work they are doing, to relate warmly and sensitively to their parishioners, and to find comfort and peace in their dealings with God. Unfortunately it sometimes takes only one need or desire left unfulfilled to spoil a priest's happiness or vocation. But the fact is, as Hoge states, there is generally more than one type of frustration responsible when a priest decides to leave the priesthood after only a few years.

A major complaint expressed by resigned priests is that their theological training did not prepare them well for coping with problems of loneliness. They were also highly critical of their preparation for celibate life.

Relative to the loneliness issue, research has found that social isolation has a powerful impact on the frequency and progression of a variety of diseases and on mortality rates. It has been shown that loneliness is a cause of heart disease, a finding that prompted cardiologist James Lynch to write, "Reflected in our hearts there is a biological basis for our need to form loving human relationships."

People who have a trusting, confiding relationship with at least one other person have been found to have lower cholesterol levels than those who lack this kind of caring support. Research has shown, too, that cancer patients often survive longer if they are blessed with the strong support of loving family members or friends.

The health of priests who experience prolonged seasons of loneliness is also threatened by the way their emotional state causes a lowered effectiveness of their body's immune mechanism. The resulting decreased production of white blood cells leaves them open to a wide array of disorders caused by bacteria, viruses, and malignant tumor cells, which are thus enabled to multiply and then overcome the priest's natural resistance to disease.

Psychological depression, too, is considered to be, in many cases, an outcome of loneliness. Moreover, research has shown that a psychotherapeutic treatment program aimed at restoring or reworking social connections and social roles can be extremely effective in treating depression—just as effective in the treatment of mild to moderate depression as antidepressant medication. A study conducted by the Rand Corporation found that individuals who share their lives with a number of close friends and relatives require mental health services significantly less frequently than those who have fewer social resources.

Living a celibate life, as viewed in Hoge's study of both active and resigned priests, has presented formidable difficulties that prevent many from finding happiness and, in some cases, success in persevering. Various authors have written about the central elements and problems related to this Church-required way of life that is characterized by a voluntary foregoing of sexual gratification for an altruistic, spiritual purpose. In my opinion, the study points out that the normal needs and desires of priests connected to relationships and celibacy have proved difficult to meet. The reason for this lapse appears to be inadequate development of social skills directly related to the seminary setting. It is usually in and through marriage that men are able to develop these skills and meet these needs and desires.

An incomplete but lengthy list of priests' often unmet celibacy-related needs (as inferred from the study) includes the following:

- a sense of belonging

- to love and feel loved

- esteem and approval

- a sense of sexual identity

- a need to feel needed

- challenged to mature

- someone to live for

- constructive feedback

- intimacy (profoundly shared experiences and feelings)

- a deeply shared common mission

- joy and playfulness

- generativity
- variety and balance in activities
- time for pleasure
- comforting compassion
- dependable moral support

The study shows that celibate priests also frequently experience unfulfilled desires. These, like unmet needs, result in frustration, anger, hostility, depression, and other painful emotions ("dysphoria" is the technical term), as described earlier. The more numerous these frustrations of needs and desires are, the more intense and long lasting, the greater the likelihood of physical or emotional illness. From a medical and psychiatric point of view, priesthood is indeed a high-risk occupation.

What can be done to preserve the health of priests and at the same time enhance their pastoral relationships and ministerial effectiveness? Seminary formation, while deserving great credit for the way so many priests learn to live pastoral lives that reflect desirable health and happiness, can, I believe, contribute significantly more than it does now to the formation of priests for the future. I would think that formators in seminaries could be more helpful to their students by assisting them to understand themselves in terms of their personal needs and help them develop skills used to meet those needs. This would first entail having each seminarian draw up a comprehensive list of his genuine needs. Then formators would help their students recognize just how they are actually meeting each need. (For example, the need for intimacy by making themselves known in depth to their friends, or the need to establish social boundaries by deliberately following predetermined ways of behaving when in the presence of women or men they find sexually attractive.)

Formators could also skillfully help their seminarians recognize their own specific desires, distinguishing them from their needs, and learn to let go of them if they cannot resourcefully find a way to fulfill them. (It is only by giving up their belief that they should get whatever they want and by ridding themselves of a sense of special entitlement that they can learn to keep anger and resentment from accumulating in their lives with the destructive consequences for their health described earlier.)

It will be important for formators, assisted by other mature and seasoned priests, to make clear to seminarians that their current needs, which are essential elements in their God-given nature, will go with them into their post-ordination lives but will often have to be met in new ways, with new resources called upon to achieve this. (For example, being a member of the student body in the seminary easily fulfills the man's sense of belonging. To meet this same need as a priest, he will have to take the initiative to regularly attend gatherings of priests, participate in retreats and workshops, and read publications designed to help priests like himself maintain their pastoral skills and fulfill their role in ministry.)

It is often reported that the transition from seminary to post-ordination life is a difficult one. Gone are the days of an always-available social group, which was a part of seminary experience. Seminary formators would do well to anticipate this situation, because it is often a time when celibacy issues rise to the fore. For instance, some men may find themselves intensely wishing they could have a wife and children. To remain celibate, seminarians need to develop a habit of deliberately setting such thinking and desiring aside while intentionally making the effort it takes to build a supportive network of collaborators and friends with whom they, as priests, can share their ministry and their lives.

The mentors and spiritual directors who will assist these men during their early years of priesthood would, I believe, do well to continue the help provided by seminary formators by keeping the priests aware of their specific human needs and assisting them to find appropriate ways to meet them. They can also call upon the wisdom they have personally acquired over years of living a fulfilling celibate life to help these younger men learn to give up the desires they cannot find a legitimate way to fulfill. This quality, which I'd like to call "realism," can make it possible to live with acceptance and peace in one's heart instead of anger, resentment, or depression.

For priests to live a celibate life successfully, the variety of human needs listed earlier must somehow be met. But issues such as sexual identity, intimacy, sexual fantasy, impulses, and feelings—all related to fundamental needs—are not usually easy for formators, spiritual directors, and mentors to bring up in conversations with seminarians and recently ordained priests. These helpers must be both knowledgeable about human sexuality and comfortable discussing issues related to sex.

I have long been convinced that persons involved in supporting the development of priests deserve and need to receive special training for this important work. For that reason, a team of us, with encouragement from a number of bishops and seminary rectors, established six years ago The Christian Institute for the Study of Human Sexuality, a month-long independent study program now located at Catholic Theological Union in Chicago. Over five hundred men and women involved in formation ministry have joined us from all over the world in an effort to better accomplish the development of our clergy and religious. Surprisingly, fewer Americans than we expected have taken advantage of this academic opportunity. My guess is that we who grow up in this country and culture have difficulty recognizing that we need, and can benefit greatly from, the help of other professionals in our efforts to accomplish our ministry well. In other words, we do not want others to see, and ourselves to be forced to acknowledge, how much remains for us to learn about human sexuality, an issue so long needed but avoided in the education and formation of our priests and religious in the Catholic Church.

Hoge's provocative study has contributed strongly to my belief that the priests whose lives are blessed with the divine gift of happiness and who successfully persevere in their calling are men whose needs and realistic desires are sufficiently fulfilled. Those who are unhappy and whose health and perseverance are endangered are usually those who feel repeatedly frustrated and disappointed. But we can improve the lives of priests (and Hoge's statistics) if we try hard enough. My suggestion: Keep our priests' needs and desires, and the skills they need to meet them, perennially in mind.

Reverend Gill is director of The Christian Institute for the Study of Human Sexuality in Chicago, Illinois, and is founder of the journal Human Development.

A Story Worth Telling

Ms. Marti R. Jewell

In the end, what sustains us are our stories. Some are the foundational stories of our faith, such as the stories told of Jesus, who chose the twelve apostles and sent out the seventy-two. Some are the stories of an early Church that designated ministries, some of which became clerical and some of which did not (Fox, p. 16). Some are the stories of the work of Jesus' followers, the work of the early Church, the Diaspora and on into the world. They are the stories of a tradition that responds to the needs of God's people, sometimes by institutionalizing ministries, as did the Council of Trent, and sometimes by renewing ministry, as did the Second Vatican Council. Yet the end of the story always remains the same. It is always about the coming of the reign of God. These are the faith stories that sustain us, even as the context in which they are told changes.

The world we live in is changing. The way we know ourselves as human beings is changing. Our perceptions of society, culture, and time have changed. Boundaries are shifting. "The implicit image of society as settled, divinely appointed, up-and-down hierarchical arrangements . . . is being replaced by horizontal imagery of 'community'" (Cooke, p. 9). The world today is better educated and more self-aware than ever before. It is a world that has come to understand that it holds within itself the power of life and death, and that it is just one small planet floating in a vast universe. It is a world that has seen scandals at every level and so no longer automatically gives trust. At the same time, it is a world where deep hunger for authentic spirituality is growing.

"Holiness is no longer defined by participation in that otherworldly realm ritually reproduced in our sanctuaries. . . . Contemporary Catholics [are] developing another sense of the sacred" (Schmitz, p. 10). People have come to discover the immanent, available nature of God and the sacramentality of ordinary life. The image of the priest, standing solitary and alone, the mediator between God and God's people has changed. A priest does not stand alone, and has not for a long time.

Parish life is flourishing, even though parishioners are not the "pray, pay, and obey" Catholics of yesterday. Sociologists are discovering that the youngest generations of Catholics differ significantly from the oldest generations in their acceptance of faith and morals (Davidson, p. 138). Parishes are expected to provide everything from childcare to schools, from sports marathons to outings for seniors. The reception of sacraments requires sacramental preparation. Many parishes require their ministers to speak multiple languages and address cross-cultural needs. And all this in a Church where the number of priests is declining by 10 percent per decade, religious by 33 percent, and parish leadership is increasingly made up of professional (or ecclesial) lay ministers. Growing at the rate of 70 percent per decade, this is the most rapidly growing segment of ministers in our Church today (Hoge, 2000).

This is the context in which we live. How, then, do we tell the story of the newly ordained? The men who are being prepared to minister in the world of the twenty-first century have a right to expect the preparation they need. A return to theologies and theories of the past will not serve them well. We do these newly ordained and the congregations they serve an injustice if we do not prepare them for today's world. The final sentences of this study are perhaps the most significant of all. A large agenda does loom ahead of us. We are learning what it means to be Church in a new era. With so much of the story changing, how do we continue to respond to the needs of God's people in ways that will serve the mission of the Church?

Practical Responses

Systems

Over the past fourteen years I have interviewed many young (and not so young) men who are applying for candidacy to the priesthood. They come with a sense of call, a desire to serve a loving God, who, they believe, has called them to the priesthood. They come to offer what they have in service to God's people. They see themselves living out this call as a personal, individual effort. Dean Hoge refers to the fact that most young priests prefer to see themselves as different, as set apart (Hoge, pp. xi–xiii).

Ministry, however, is not an individual effort. It does not, in fact cannot, happen in isolation. It is the action of the entire faith community responding to the presence of a loving God. Ministry is about the building up of the kingdom, about faith communities that care for one another and carry the Good News into the world. In today's Church, ordained serve our Church community alongside lay ecclesial ministers, men and women who believe they have a vocation to service within the Church (*Spiritual Formation,* p. 30). The newly ordained do not stand alone. They are moving into a ministerial community, which must respect what they bring and which asks for that same respect in return. Lay and ordained roles are different, but the life of the Church is supported by such a ministerial community. How do we establish role clarity for both the ordained and the lay ecclesial minister? Leaders of parish communities, ordained and lay alike, must hold the vision and model the actions that support the life of the Church.

Socialization

Education for ministry goes far beyond the communication of specific theological knowledge. It is a complex and lifelong process that demands adjustments that can range from mild to severe (Yunker, p. 2). New ministers, whether ordained or lay ecclesial ministers, have much to learn as they are socialized into their roles in the Church. While new ministers can quickly discover some of the basic information they need, such as how to reserve the parish hall or how to complete sacramental records, there is another area of socialization that is much subtler and far less easy to discover.

New ministers are entering a world that has its own culture, its own language, beliefs, traditions, and attitudes. How do they learn this culture? How does the newly ordained come to deal with the fact that he is no longer a private person but has become a public figure? How do they understand how to cope with being either deified or vilified by those they serve? How do they learn to minister in a theologically diverse Church?

What has become the norm inside a closed seminary or academic community—for example, styles of clothing, expressions of sexual orientation, or personal piety—may not be appropriate in a parish community. It can be challenging to move from an "ivory tower" environment with its own culture, systems, and relationships into a diocesan and parish structure that is quite different and often far less nurturing.

How do ministers, ordained and lay, learn to collaborate with one another? Often when newly ordained move into a parish structure, they will be working with seasoned and experienced lay ministers who are the decision-makers in their particular arena. How do the newly ordained learn to be supervisors? There are situations when a lay person, as likely to be female as male, becomes the supervisor of the ordained. How do new ministers learn about gender differences and how to work with colleagues of the opposite sex? How do they learn servant leadership with its call to serve and empower rather than be in charge?

The entry experiences of the newly ordained, paralleled by those of new lay ecclesial ministers, reflect a period of disillusionment. How the new minister is initiated into the diocesan and parish structures will, for good or ill, impact his ministry, life, and service for years to come.

Collaboration

"One challenge undergirds all of the above. It is the need to foster respectful collaboration, leading to mutual support in ministry, between clergy and laity for the sake of Christ's Church and its mission to the world. This is a huge task requiring changes in patterns of reflection, behavior, and expectation among laity and clergy alike" (*Called and Gifted*, p. 18). New ministers need to have experiences of healthy, collaborative parishes. A healthy workplace is one in which people know how to listen to one another, can be truthful with one another, work well with diverse members, and have free access to one another and to needed information. It is one in which collaboration is truly honored (Wheatley, p. 40). We can learn from those who are successfully accomplishing this collaboration. "The ministry of the ordained and the ministry of ecclesial lay ministers are mutually supportive and essential to the work of the kingdom of God. Effective collaboration is life-giving to both lay ministers and ordained ministers but gives its greatest gift to those who receive its greatest benefit: the entire people of God" (Joint Letter, p. 2).

Implications

1. There is a need to further develop our theology of ministry.

According to Father Michael Himes, "Crucial to a renewal of ordained priesthood in our time is a renewal of the priesthood of the whole Church. Unless the priesthood of the laity is fostered, the priesthood of the ordained must languish" (Himes, p. 8). As we minister to the people of God, we are called to patterns of relationship that honor both ordained and lay ecclesial ministers, standing shoulder to shoulder in their service to the mission of the Church. The voices, roles, and significance of lay ecclesial ministers are missing in this study. Yet the bishops, as recently as 1999, have called the Church to value and develop the relationship between lay and ordained ecclesial ministers (p. 43). While lay ecclesial ministers are professionals in every sense of that word, to view their presence as "paid staff" or as "lay involvement" is to miss the crucial new chapter in the story of the Church. Lay ecclesial ministers serve from a sense of vocation.

Our understanding of both sacraments and Scripture support this development. "Central to the renewed concept of ministry in general and lay ministry specifically is the council's definition of the Church as the 'People of God.' . . . It presents the scriptural image of the human and communal nature of the Church where all baptized are members of the community.

All members share in the ministry of Jesus, whether ordained or not. Baptism is seen as the defining sacrament of ministry" (Reynolds, pp. 23–24). The parable, offered in *Christifideli Laici,* of the vineyard owner who called workers at different hours of the day, yet offered the same work and the same wages, serves as a powerful model (John Paul II, p. 4). Models for shared ministry are found in Paul's letters to the Corinthians with their theology of the Body of Christ. Lay ecclesial ministry, flowing in its present form from the Second Vatican Council, is grounded in a theology of an image as ancient as that of hierarchy (Whitehead, p. 31).

"In the wake of the Council we have arrived at a clearer recognition that it is in the nature of the Church to be endowed with many gifts. . . . All ministry, be it the ministry of the baptized or of the ordained, is to be understood in relation to the community of the Church which expresses and receives its identity as the Body of Christ in Word and sacrament. All ministry is for the service of the Church and the wider world, a participation in the ministry of Christ the servant" (Mahony, pp. 746–747). The relationship of the ordained and the lay minister, one of *communio,* flowing from baptism and rooted in the ministry of Jesus, has become the unfolding story of ministry in the Church today.

2. Second, there is a need to deepen our understanding of the sacramental life of the Church.

Stories that continue to sustain us have an underlying rhythm that holds them together. With time, the rhythm becomes more complex, richer, and multi-layered. The stories of the Catholic Church are held together by the rhythm of our sacramental nature, a rhythm that has developed over time. We are a sacramental Church. Cardinal Danneels, writing to the Synod of Bishops, says that people long for the sacraments and yet do not appreciate their meaning (Danneels, p. 6). Perhaps what is happening is that people are listening to the ever more complex rhythms in our sacramental life. The sacramental life of the Church, like ministry, is found in the context of the faith community. We have come to know ourselves as a eucharistic people, the Body of Christ. We believe that baptism is the source of all ministry. How are we telling the stories of the future of the Church? How do we reconcile the impact of fewer ordinations on the sacramental life of the Church? We are a eucharistic people. How do we sustain this most basic rhythm of our story?

Conclusion

In the words of Dean Hoge, the mission continues but the circumstances are changing. The faces, the parishioners, the ministers are different. We are called to be a healing, ministering, evangelizing presence in the world. We are forming ministerial communities of ordained and lay ecclesial ministers, working together, integrally woven into the Body of Christ, called by vocation, calling forth the community of believers, a community, in turn, called to minister to the world. The bishops have begun the dialogue that is essential to the process. Seminaries and academic programs have a significant role to play. Conversations between lay and ordained ministers are taking place in parishes, dioceses, and on the national level. What is ahead of us, in the words of Bishop Howard Hubbard, ". . . is not some sort of tragic ecclesial catastrophe, but a deepening and broadening of awareness about the nature of the Church as a community of collaborative ministry and about the authentic nature of priestly service" (Hubbard, p. 3). Can we create the stories that will call forth and empower those needed by our Church today? It is an agenda worth taking on, a story worth telling.

Bibliography

Castelli, James, and Eugene Hemrick. "National Catholic Parish Survey: The New Church Emerges." Fairfax, Va.: Castelli Enterprises, 2000.

Cooke, Bernard. "Wind of Change." *National Catholic Reporter,* August 9, 1996.

Danneels, Godfried. "The Contemporary Person and the Church: An Intervention at the Consistory." *America,* July 30–August 6, 2001.

Davidson, James. *The Search for Common Ground: What Unites and Divides Catholic Americans.* Our Sunday Visitor, 1997.

Fox, Zeni. "Laity in Leadership Roles in the Church in the United States Today: A Theological and Pastoral Overview." Paper called for by Fadica, 2000.

Granfield, Patrick. "The Concept of the Church as Communion." *Origins,* vol. 28, no. 44 (April 22, 1999).

Himes, Michael J. "Making Priesthood Possible: Who Does What and Why." *Church.* New York: National Pastoral Life Center (Fall, 1989).

Hoge, Dean R. "New Catholic Leadership: What Does It Mean to Be a Catholic in 2000?" Address given at the Conference for Pastoral Planning and Council Development, Boston, April 2, 2000.

Hubbard, Howard. "Continental Congress on Vocations." *Crux of the News* (July 9, 2001).

John Paul II. "The Vocation and the Mission of the Lay Faithful in the Church and in the World: *Christifideles Laici.*" Post-synodal apostolic exhortation (December 30, 1988). Boston: St. Paul Books and Media, 1988.

Joint Letter to the Subcommittee on Lay Ministry from the National Association for Lay Ministry and the National Federation of Priests Councils (June, 1998).

Mahony, Roger. "Pastoral Letter on Ministry: As I Have Done for You." *Origins,* vol. 29, no. 46 (May 4, 2000).

National Conference of Catholic Bishops. Bishops' Committee on the Laity. *Called and Gifted for the Third Millennium: Reflections of the U.S. Catholic Bishops* on the Thirtieth Anniversary of the Decree on the Apostolate of the Laity and the Fifteenth Anniversary of Called and Gifted. Publication 5-002. Washington: United States Catholic Conference, 1995.

National Conference of Catholic Bishops. Subcommittee on Lay Ministry, Committee on the Laity. *Lay Ecclesial Ministry: The State of the Questions*. Publication 5-345. Washington: United States Catholic Conference, 1999.

Reynolds, Brian B. "The Development of Pastoral Administrators in Catholic Parishes in the United States." Dissertation, Spalding University, Louisville, Ky. (1999).

Schmitz, Robert E. "Of Dinosaurs, Carrier Pigeons, and Disappearing Priests." *America* (October 12, 1996).

United States Conference of Catholic Bishops. *Spiritual Formation of Lay Ecclesial Ministers*. Washington: United States Catholic Conference, 2001.

Wheatley, Margaret. *Leadership and the New Science: Discovering Order in a Chaotic World*. San Francisco: Barrett-Koehler, 1999.

Whitehead, James D. "Christian Images of Community: Power and Leadership." In *Alternative Futures for Leadership* 6 (1987).

Yunker, Rose. "Professional Socialization Programs: Texts and Subtexts." Ministry Educators in Conversation: Invitational Conference, February 4–7, 1993, San Antonio, Tex.

Ms. Jewell is director of the Office of Ministry and Spirituality for the Archdiocese of Louisville. She serves as member and past chair of the board of directors of the National Association for Lay Ministry. Her ministry focuses primarily on the professional and spiritual formation of ministers.

The Need for Connections

Rev. Stephen J. Rossetti, Ph.D., D.Min.

In recent years, we at Saint Luke Institute, a residential treatment program for clergy and religious, have noticed that we are receiving some referrals to evaluate and treat newly ordained priests, some not even ordained for a year. This is a new phenomenon and one that bears reflection. These men, young in the priesthood, are coming to us with a variety of personal issues, such as substance abuse, sexual difficulties, depression, and/or chronic interpersonal problems.

Since the Institute has not yet engaged in a direct study of these referrals, there are no definitive answers that would explain this phenomenon. However, the answers will likely be complex and involve a variety of societal trends, such as the breakdown of the nuclear family, a rising societal awareness of psychological problems, and a wider social acceptance of engaging in psychotherapy.

At the same time, there are probably some issues that are directly related to the priesthood and the Church. With the reduced numbers of vocations, it is possible that a few candidates are slipping through the process and being ordained who in previous days might not have been. One hears such anecdotal stories fairly often, although most in formation work would agree that the bulk of the candidates for the priesthood today are solid psychologically and spiritually.

Most important, it appears that our young priests are placed in situations of great stress with few personal supports. I was recently in conversation with a priest-psychologist from South America. He described the situation in his country, where newly ordained priests are often put in a parochial setting of tens of thousands of the faithful and there are few, if any, other priests for guidance and support. These newly ordained are simply swamped and overwhelmed, both psychologically and spiritually.

While the situation in the United States is not quite as severe, the same dynamics are present. There are few younger priests with whom to form a social network; there are fewer older priests available as informal mentors; newly ordained are sometimes made pastors of parishes after only a few years of experience; and the needs and demands of parochial ministry are relentless, often unrealistic, and growing.

In fairness to our formation programs and to our dioceses and religious orders, these trends are well known and programs are being put into place to cope with these new realities. We see the rise of mentoring programs for newly ordained. Many dioceses require the newly ordained to meet regularly as a group to share their experiences and to support one another. Most dioceses work hard at making the priest's first assignment as good as possible by finding a good first pastor for a mentor and a supportive parish. Nevertheless, the aforementioned trends remain, and they stress the health and vocations of our newly ordained.

This is coupled with what I believe is a rising negativity toward priestly vocations. Celibacy is questioned within and without the Church, which cannot but negatively influence the resolve of our young priests to live a faithful celibate life. Also, the Catholic Church continues to come under attack from the "Left" and the "Right," as well as from some feminists and the media. The Church is criticized for maintaining an all-male priesthood. Recent media releases question the integrity of the priesthood and its health. Under all this negative pressure, the "Bells of Saint Mary's" and the days when it was considered a blessing to have a son as a priest are relegated to an era long past. With all these trends within and without the Church, the fact that any men present themselves for ordination and persevere in the priesthood ought to be seen as another sign of the miracle of God's grace.

The findings of Dr. Dean Hoge, in this excellent study commissioned by the National Federation of Priests' Councils (NFPC), are illuminating and important. The results help us to understand not only why some priests leave the ministry after only a few years but also why some priests remain. I believe that many of his findings in this study can be summed up in the concept of "connection." Most of those priests who left the active priesthood did not feel connected to the Church, their pastors, or to other priests. Often they felt lonely, isolated, and unappreciated. It is obvious to assert that lonely and isolated people are much more likely to exhibit clinical symptoms and concomitant spiritual problems. They are more likely to leave the active ministry or come to Saint Luke Institute.

An important question, which might be the grist for a follow-up study, is why some priests can be put in the midst of an active, demanding ministry and find the connections necessary to live a happy and productive celibate life while others cannot. It has long been our experience at Saint Luke's that the ability of our priests to form peer relationships is key to both psychological and spiritual health. Much of our work is helping priests to learn to connect with others and with their God. Isolation breeds discontent and dysfunction. If seminaries were able to employ only one criterion to signal readiness for ordination, I believe it should be the ability of the seminarian to form relationships. I am reminded of the saying in the First Letter of John: "For whoever does not love a brother or sister whom he has seen cannot love God whom he has not seen" (4:20).

Similarly, *Pastores Dabo Vobis,* the Pope's apostolic exhortation on formation for the priesthood, speaks of "human formation" as the "necessary foundation" upon which all other aspects of priestly formation depend. The Holy Father wrote: "Of special importance is the capacity to relate to others. This is truly fundamental for a person who is called to be responsible for a community and to be a 'man of communion.'" Dr. Hoge's study statistically affirms the Holy Father's insight.

This NFPC study also suggested differences between the spiritual lives of the priests who stayed and those who left. I found these differences particularly intriguing. Both groups felt a strong and satisfying relationship with the laity whom they served. They enjoyed administering the sacraments, preaching, helping people, and being a part of their lives. But the two groups differed in their relationship to the Catholic Church and in their perception of their vocations. The majority of the group that stayed in active ministry (54%) felt "being a visible sign of the Catholic Church" was of great importance, 48% were very satisfied with their relationship with their bishop, and a large majority (72%) saw their vocations as "a response to the divine call." For the resigned group, the numbers were 28%, 22%, and 47% respectively, a substantial decline.

These numbers should be important points for reflection both in seminaries and in presbyterates. The priest is not a "private practitioner." He is not a lone ranger who works in isolation, doing "his ministry." Rather, the priesthood is radically communitarian. The priesthood, if it is lived well, becomes a united body of priests, called by God, gathered together around their bishop, and sharing in the Church's ministry.

How does a formation program instill such values? These will be difficult to inculcate. They imply such attributes as humility, obedience, listening, prayerfulness, docility, and fraternal charity. I am reminded of the words of a few young priests who left the ministry after being upset by what they perceived as a Church that had become too "liberal." They said, "I didn't leave the Church. The Church left me." On the other extreme, some young priests have left because they disagreed with the Church on a number of doctrinal and pastoral issues and believed that it has become too "conserva-tive." In both cases one senses a lack of trust in the Holy Spirit's guidance of the Church, a certain personal willfulness, and a lack of docility.

It is no accident that our experience at Saint Luke Institute suggests that recovery for our clients is never on solid ground until they have regained a strong connection with their spiritual lives and their ecclesial roots. Faith, by its very nature, has a communal dimension and achieves its fruition in a body of believers, led by the Holy Spirit. The priest is an official represen-tative of the Catholic Church, and he is called to be so by his bishop, as head of the local church, but animating that call is a vocation from God. These must be part of the identity of our priests.

It is important to recognize what this study has addressed and what it has not. It has begun to look at why some priests leave the active ministry, and it investigated possible causes within the priesthood and the Church it-self. It did not address larger societal changes that are likely to have a pro-found, albeit more subtle, effect on priestly resignations. In fact, one might make the case that a larger percentage of the variance in why more priests are resigning in recent years is due to trends outside the Church.

In days gone by, when people made lifetime commitments in our so-ciety, they were expected to honor these commitments regardless of whether they felt "happy" about their state in life or not. Thus, in marriage, people rarely divorced; it was largely unheard of, and it was a scandal when they did. Statistics on divorce suggest that a rising percentage of people in the United States are getting divorced, many in the first few years after mar-riage. It seems obvious that there are megatrends in society that are affect-ing divorce rates, priests leaving ministry, and other similar phenomena. It would be misleading to view this study in isolation and conclude that these increased numbers of resignations are completely unique to the priesthood. While this does not negate the vital information in this study, such findings will be misleading if not viewed in its larger context.

We, as Church, should be grateful to NFPC and Dr. Hoge for the impor-tant findings in this study. It ought to be mandatory reading for formators, seminary faculties, and presbyteral councils. Nevertheless, I have a con-cern about how these statistics will be used. There are a few who tend to be naysayers. They decry the current state of the Church and assert that it is on the road to collapse. Closely allied to this group are those who believe the priesthood is fundamentally dysfunctional and fatally flawed. This is not my experience. The priesthood and the Catholic Church in this country are strong. As I attend Catholic churches on Sunday mornings around this country and meet with presbyterates from diocese to diocese, I continue to be edified by the faith of the people, the strength of our parishes, and the courage of our priests.

Nevertheless, we are not perfect, and this study has pointed out some avenues for improvement. It is my sincere hope that we seize the moment and work more diligently to screen and form our candidates for the priesthood well and to make the first few years of their priesthood the best experience possible. Ultimately we will want to foster priestly "connections." Our goal is to form a community of priests who are connected to each other, to the people whom they serve, to the universal Church, and to the God who has called them.

Reverend Rossetti is a priest of the diocese of Syracuse and president and chief executive officer of Saint Luke Institute in Silver Spring, Maryland.

The Study's Implications for Seminary Formators

Sr. Katarina Schuth, O.S.F.

The vast array of data presented in this study of newly ordained priests opens up numerous possibilities for observations and reflections, such as the unmistakable differences between active and resigned priests, and the contrast between religious and diocesan priests. My approach, based on some of the key findings, is to suggest ways of reversing negative situations that contribute to the dissatisfaction of active priests and the resignation of others. The major findings present issues in four broad categories:

- vocational discernment and selection
- seminary formation programs
- placements and pastoral ministry
- presbyteral and community relationships.

These comments focus on the first two sets of findings, with the goal of identifying effective practices relating to discernment and formation that might lead to greater satisfaction and higher retention of newly ordained priests. Bishops and religious superiors, pastors, vocation directors, and seminary faculties all have something to contribute to ensuring more positive outcomes. Ultimately every Church member will benefit from improved practices.

Some Major Findings Concerning Vocational Discernment and Selection

- Before seminary, nearly three-fourths of seminarians experienced a spiritual awakening; two-thirds found it important in their vocational discernment.

- Positive relationships with priests and religious were often key factors in the decision to consider the priesthood.

- A remarkable number of priests are sons of alcoholic fathers or mothers who were dominant in their lives.

- Some priests experienced strong parental pressure for them to enter the priesthood.

Implications Relating to Vocational Discernment and Selection

These findings concern common factors that influence seminarians in their vocational choice. One addresses internal motivation, and several others relate to external factors. First is the reality that a large number of seminarians have experienced a spiritual awakening. This study and corroborating research suggest that considerable consequences for formation and future ministry follow. Among these seminarians, some have converted from one or another Christian denomination, but more typically the phenomenon is one of reconversion. The latter group, though baptized Catholic at birth, have been away from the Church for many years. One factor precipitating their vocational call was a significant prayer experience, for example, during a pilgrimage to Medjugorie or at a large religious gathering. Another source of awakening was an invitation by a charismatic person, typically a priest, who may have asked them if they had ever considered priesthood, which they interpreted as a sign from God. Still others were impressed by an individual's commitment and dedication, and wished to follow in his or her footsteps. The common thread is a somewhat abrupt shift in their relationship with God and Church.

Depending on the nature of the conversion experience and the convert's age at the time, the impact varies: the older the candidate and the more dramatic the conversion, the greater the obstacles to religious development. Because of the rather sudden shift in their life direction, these seminarians more often than not have minimal knowledge of Catholic culture, may have enjoyed only a short-term or sporadic association with a parish, and lack familiarity with the diocese for which they plan to be ordained. Their roots within the Catholic community are often shallow.

Vocation directors and seminary formation faculty need to take seriously this phenomenon. They might expect that the experience of transition and change in their spiritual lives would lead these candidates to be flexible and open to change. Instead, it often leads to rigidity born of a desire for security and stability. The relative lack of religious background and knowledge of the Church's tradition can make them vulnerable—afraid of disturbing their new-found insights in the desire to maintain the fervor they have gained from their recent religious experience. This attitude can turn into fear of new knowledge about their faith that will, from their perspective, obliterate their spiritual life.

Vocation directors who are attentive to the intensity of the spiritual awakening and how it affects the vocational choice will be able to help candidates work through the changes necessary to engage in the formation process. During the period of discernment future seminarians need to be exposed to the richness and variety of the Catholic tradition. They might do this by visiting an array of parishes with varied approaches to ministry, by working with a spiritual director who will challenge some of their assumptions, and by meeting with others who are in the process of discernment. Readiness for theological studies makes all the difference in the depth of spiritual development that can take place. Formation faculty who are aware of the spiritual histories of seminarians can guide them toward a secure faith that brings freedom and peace as they pursue priesthood.

Familial and other personal relationships in the early life of candidates are also significant in their decisions to enter the seminary. Familial influence as a motivation for priesthood is complicated. Some priests said they felt excessive pressure from their parents, whether in the form of trying to "make up for the sins of an alcoholic father," pleasing a dominant mother, or giving in to the keen desire of the family to have a son as a priest. Supportive relationships with priests and religious can serve to bolster the decision to enter seminary and encourage movement toward priesthood. They may also be helpful in promoting an understanding of what the calling entails, thus making the transition to ministry less dissonant. On the negative side, prospective candidates whose vocational decisions are attached too closely to one or another person rather than being internal to the candidate can lack the necessary grounding for long-term commitment.

Vocation directors must do careful screening to help candidates discern between an authentic internal call as opposed to a response coming from undue external influence. For the sake of larger numbers, the temptation in recent years has been to urge hasty movement toward a vocational decision that in the long run is counterproductive. Allowing the proper time for maturation of the call is critical. Later on formation directors who help seminarians understand their initial motivation and then encourage them to deepen their commitment or leave the seminary if they cannot do so contribute significantly to the permanence of the vocational choice. Given the frequency of troubled family backgrounds of seminarians, seminary faculties would benefit from more knowledge about the psychological impact of issues such as being adult children of alcoholics. These recommendations are useful in two ways: they sharpen the discernment process and focus formation issues common to entering seminarians.

Some Major Findings Concerning Formation Programs

- In evaluating their theological seminary experience, respondents rated *very favorably* formal theological training, homiletics, spirituality and prayer life, and pastoral care and counseling. Nonetheless, active priests strongly recommend development of a stronger prayer life during seminary.

- The priests rated *somewhat favorably* balancing self-care and ministry, working with lay staff, handling multiple tasks and responsibilities, and working with multiple ethnic groups. At the same time they had strong concerns about burnout and overwork, and they wished they could have had more experience interacting with women.

- They rated *very unfavorably* training in church administration. To correct the deficiency, they strongly recommended more practical, hands-on training and more realistic parish experiences during formation, including having a pastoral year away from the seminary.

- Many respondents believed that seminaries should discuss more openly sexuality in general and topics such as celibacy and homosexuality in particular, indicating that discussion needs to take place in classes and in formation programs and personal counseling.

Implications Relating to Formation Programs

Faculty who provide human and spiritual formation and those who are responsible for intellectual and academic formation need to be alert to the changing formational needs of seminarians. The findings of this study are encouraging in that newly ordained priests report positively about most areas of their formation, as identified above. These key dimensions of formation are essential to the success of their future ministry and to their satisfaction with priesthood. Yet even as the survey was laudatory about how well prepared they were in some areas, other parts of formation were judged somewhat deficient or underemphasized, namely, church administration, dealing with celibacy and loneliness, and the overall environment of the seminary.

The area of seminary formation that received the lowest rating was preparation for church administration. The newly ordained felt that the courses and experiences of the seminary were not adequate for them to take on these responsibilities. Research suggests several possible explanations. First of all, seminaries are hard-pressed to include any more areas of study than are already required by the Program of Priestly Formation and the requests of various bishops and religious superiors. Consider also that in recent years seminarians have come from backgrounds that did not include much experience with the Church and parish life. Further, their apprenticeship years as an associate pastor have been radically reduced. Finally, if courses in administrative practices are offered, they are not always productive in the more or less abstract classroom setting.

How can the problem be addressed? It is conceivable that seminarians could spend more time in parishes during studies and be assigned to an internship year with careful supervision. However, bishops eager to have men ordained more quickly are not always keen on another year of preparation. As an alternative, pastors could be given assistance in mentoring so that they would be better able to introduce newly ordained priests to the main responsibilities of the office. Dioceses could also be proactive in providing lengthier required training for newly appointed pastors. These suggestions are difficult to implement because of the growing shortage of priests and the immense demands on their time. Yet in the long run it would be productive in helping priests with the transition to full responsibility for church administration. Additionally, lay parish administrators are of enormous assistance in many parishes and their services could be more fully utilized.

The research shows that a significant concern of newly ordained priests is dealing with celibacy and loneliness and with combining priesthood with love and intimacy. Further, those who have left active ministry say it is the main cause for their resignation. The report states that "the study was suffused with talk about celibacy, loneliness, desire for intimacy, and homosexuality—more so than we expected." Findings of this sort often lead to criticism of seminary formation, suggesting that human and spiritual preparation is absent or inadequate. Having examined in detail every American seminary formation program, the criticism, it seems to me, is by and large unfounded. In the past ten to fifteen years major improvements were made in formation that help seminarians comprehend the meaning of celibacy and understand themselves as sexual persons, as well as in encouraging them to develop support networks and to handle problems of loneliness.

So why the concern? First of all, it is possible that too much of formation is intellectually oriented. This comment from the study supports the contention: "Make sure people are in touch with their heart. I think I made my decisions from my head. I don't think there was much about my formation in seminary, as good as it was, that truly led me to my heart." Toward this goal, formation directors might urge seminarians to meet with psychological counselors to help explore these issues and, as many do, require clinical pastoral education during seminary.

Further, what is taught is not always what is learned. Some seminarians are unable or unwilling to engage in serious discussion about these important matters. They may be threatened by the challenges that formation faculty introduce. Formation faculty in turn may be concerned about student reactions and pull back from frankly addressing the concerns. The research findings support this supposition. While about three-fourths of those who are active priests felt they were very well or well prepared in matters concerning sexuality, intimacy, and loneliness, only about half of those who resigned felt that way. These data suggest that the majority of programs meet the needs of seminarians, but some do not. The present study is unable to discern whether it was an inadequate program or an unreceptive student that was responsible for the unsatisfactory results. Since it is such a major factor in resignations, research on the retention rates of each seminary would be informative.

Finally, the survey showed that some newly ordained priests believed that the seminary environment should be altered so it is more a foretaste of what a priest's life will be and less an all-encompassing and secure home. Two changes are suggested in the study's narrative. First is concern about living situations after ordination, which many priests find less than desirable. Perhaps their views of older priests and their way of life were idealized, or, more likely, their own new role as associate or subordinate requires a different relationship that is less than pleasing. What could be done in the seminary to address this concern? Two possibilities: seminarians could spend more time living in rectories before ordination to gain a better sense of what the reality is, and while in the seminary they could be given more responsibility for their own well-being and more independence as they approach ordination.

Another matter concerns relationships with women. The study states: "Whereas women were not present in the seminary, in the parish they were everywhere. In the parish the young priests were working hand-in-hand with women in putting on church programs." While many seminaries enroll women in their programs, others do not, or the women and lay men are enrolled in entirely separate programs. Many bishops seem to prefer the latter arrangements, while religious superiors generally support the combined program.

In light of this reality, what might seminaries for diocesan students do to compensate for the structure? The most common practice is to encourage field education programs that ensure interaction with women on parish staffs and with a wide range of parishioners. Further, many seminary faculties include a significant proportion of women who participate fully in the formation process. The extent of exposure to women varies widely and so too the assessment of this issue by the newly ordained.

Conclusion

The study explored numerous dimensions of the lives of priests ordained in the past five years. Most remain in the priesthood and are immensely satisfied with their ministry and with the ways they were prepared for it. At the same time the priests who have resigned and those who are active identified some areas for improvement. This commentary concerned itself with findings related to vocational discernment and formation, suggesting that the background of seminarians and their motivations for priesthood need to be dealt with before and during formation if they are to be free and secure in their commitment to priesthood. During seminary formation, awareness of their own personal needs and development and realism about their future ministry are of primary importance if they are to live as dedicated and effective priests, deeply rooted in prayer and a spiritual life that is essential to ministry.

Sister Schuth is a faculty member and researcher at the Saint Paul Seminary, School of Divinity, University of St. Thomas, St. Paul, Minnesota.

Pastorally Effective?

Br. Loughlan Sofield, S.T.

A well-known theologian, when asked about his reaction to the perennial debate of conservative versus liberal, responded, "There is only one valid question: Is the person pastorally effective?" That question served as the backdrop as I reflected on this study. As I read about the priests ordained for less than five years, I attempted to picture them as they were revealed in this study and evaluate them in terms of their ability to be pastorally effective.

Pastoral effectiveness is a subjective term. Therefore, I would like to propose three criteria for fostering pastoral effectiveness:

- Priests must be relational.

- The primary concern of the priest should be to be an evangelizing leader.

- Any priest who will be effective today must be able to minister collaboratively.

These criteria, though, are not just my private beliefs. Pope John Paul II, Pope Paul VI, the United States Conference of Catholic Bishops, and Cardinal Roger Mahony, to name just a few, have commented on these criteria.

Pope John Paul II unequivocally stated the need for pastoral ministers to be relational when, in speaking about seminary formation, he indicated that "of special importance is the capacity to relate to others. This is truly fundamental for a person who is called to be responsible for a community and to be a 'man of communion.'"[1]

---

[1] Pope John Paul II. *I Will Give You Shepherds (Pastores Dabo Vobis)*. Boston: St. Paul Books and Media, 1992, no. 43.

Both Pope Paul VI and Pope John Paul II stressed the importance of the Church being an instrument of evangelization. Pope Paul VI has equated evangelization with the very essence of the Church: "Evangelization is in fact the grace and vocation proper to the Church, her deepest identity."[2] Pope John Paul II has indicated that the Church will be successful in implementing its call to evangelization only to the degree that it becomes more collaborative: "In order to meet the contemporary demands of evangelization, the collaboration of the laity is becoming more and more indispensable."[3]

The United States Conference of Catholic Bishops has spoken on the urgency of collaborative ministry: "For the Church, collaboration is not an option. . . . Collaboration is a means for becoming who God wants us to be,"[4] and, again, they counsel that "the Church's pastoral ministry can be more effective if we become true collaborators."[5]

Cardinal Roger Mahony, in an insightful and prophetic pastoral letter, compared the parish of 1955 with the parish we can anticipate in 2005. He clearly describes the fact that there is no comparison between these two parishes. He indicates that those attempting to minister as they did in the past will be completely ineffective if they refuse to be collaborative. He declares that "ministry in the new millennium will be more collaborative and more inclusive in its exercise."[6]

The study raised numerous issues. I limited myself to a single question, "How effective will these newly ordained priests, as described in this research, be as leaders in this collaborative Church?" The research clearly identifies a number of issues that must be addressed if they are to be effective, pastoral, collaborative leaders.

- Attitudes that militate against collaboration must be eradicated.

- They will need to be more relational.

- They must be filled with life.

---

[2] Pope Paul VI. *On Evangelization in the Modern World (Evangelii Nuntiandi).* Washington: United States Catholic Conference, 1975, no. 14.

[3] Pope John Paul II. Address to the Oblates of St. Joseph, February 17, 2000. *L'Osservatore Romano,* Weekly edition, March 2, 2000, p. 6.

[4] National Conference of Catholic Bishops. Committee on Women in Society and in the Church. *From Words to Deeds: Continuing Reflections on the Role of Women in the Church.* Washington: United States Catholic Conference, 1998, pp. 18–21.

[5] National Conference of Catholic Bishops. Bishops' Committee on the Laity. *Called and Gifted for the Third Millennium: Reflections of the U.S. Catholic Bishops on the Thirtieth Anniversary of the Decree on the Apostolate of the Laity and the Fifteenth Anniversary of Called and Gifted.* Publication 5-002. Washington: United States Catholic Conference, 1995.

[6] Roger Mahony. "Pastoral Letter on Ministry: As I Have Done for You." *Origins,* vol. 29, no. 46 (May 4, 2000) 741–753.

Attitudes That Militate Against Collaboration

I have been blessed to conduct continuing education programs for clergy in many dioceses both in the United States and in other countries around the world. I am constantly impressed with the conviction of most priests of the need for collaborative ministry. Their desire to acquire the skills needed to foster greater collaboration is also most evident. However, they are quick to admit that their seminary training did little or nothing to provide them with the skills and processes to foster collaboration.

This research raises serious questions about whether the next generation of pastors will have this same conviction of the need for collaborative ministry. What is especially disheartening is the prevailing attitudes and beliefs of many of these men that militate against any possible collaboration. This is most evident in Table A6 (p. 172). Thirty-six percent of diocesan priests agree strongly or moderately with the statement that "Catholic laity need to be better educated to respect the authority of the priest's word." Sixty-nine percent agree with the statement "A priest must see himself as a 'man set apart' by God." The statement that "ordination confers on a priest a new status which makes him essentially different from the laity" received 75 percent agreement. And finally, 43 percent agree that "it is essential to make the distinction between priests and laity more important in the Church."

Taken individually, any one of these statements might not be objectionable. However, it is the cumulative combination of these beliefs that raises serious concerns about whether these men would see any value or need to collaborate.

The United States Conference of Catholic Bishops states that the first practical step in implementing collaboration is to examine one's attitudes and behaviors.[7] Behaviors follow attitudes. The attitudes evidenced by the above statements ensure that collaboration will not occur when these men are in leadership roles unless there is a drastic change in their attitudes.

Developing One's Relational Ability

One of the characteristics of good ministry is that it is relational. Most people report experiencing ministry in the context of some relationship with the minister. It is not so much what one does for another as the way one is in relationship with the other that results in ministry. The capacity to be relational is even more important in collaborative ministry, which requires ongoing dialogue and frequent interaction with the others with whom one ministers.

The priests described in this study do not generally appear to be men who possess a great capacity for relationships. Many of them seem incapable of

---

[7] Committee on Women in Society and in the Church.

dealing constructively with loneliness, affection, love, and celibacy. As the study concluded, "Our study was suffused with talk about celibacy, loneliness, desire for intimacy and homosexuality." The main reason offered by the resigned priests for leaving was their inability to successfully resolve these issues. From what is revealed in the study, it could be concluded that many priests who have remained have not successfully mastered these psycho-sexual developmental tasks. Failure to do so severely restricts their ability to be relational and therefore to be effective in ministry in general, and in collaborative ministry specifically. One is left wondering if the relatively small number of active priests who perceive living a celibate life or dealing with loneliness as a problem (7 percent and 8 percent respectively) are in denial.

The study reports that there were a "remarkable" number of priests who had alcoholic fathers. In describing such people, it identifies certain characteristics that are the antithesis of successful relational ministers:

- They suffer from interpersonal problems.

- They exhibit high anxiety about intimacy.

- They frequently distance themselves emotionally.

- They have a fear of attachments.

- They learn to anticipate mistrust in relationships.

- They have a fear of making themselves vulnerable or of being abandoned.

- Although they desire love and intimacy, their experiences of the past block them from entering into meaningful relationships.

Given this profile, it becomes easily apparent that these men will be prone to eschew relationships. Since collaborative ministry demands the capacity to be relational, it follows that they will make very poor collaborative leaders. Even those who overcome their reluctance and have the courage to attempt collaboration will probably experience failure because they have not developed the capacity for intimacy and relationships.

Being Filled with Life

The statistics are clear. The number of priests is decreasing at between 10 and 20 percent per decade and will continue to do so into the foreseeable future. At the same time that the Church is experiencing a reduction in the number of priests, the number of Catholics is increasing at about 10 percent per decade. We can expect that the expectations on priests will increase rather than decrease as each priest finds the ratio between himself and the number of Catholics he has pastoral responsibility for increasing.

As the study predicts, "Clearly the parish as we have known it cannot continue to be maintained in the future." Effective pastoral ministry will require a radical ministerial approach. That approach, I conclude, is to foster collaboration, animating the gifts of the entire Christian community. The leaders must embrace the conviction that "we are the Church." Embracing that conviction leads to the realization that everyone shares in the responsibility for fostering the mission of Jesus Christ. Priests who will be effective leaders in this approach must be filled with life. However, the picture that emerged was of the newly ordained experiencing more burnout than life. Consider the following:

- The narratives were peppered with indications of what the individual priest "did." The litany of tasks was long and conveyed a greater sense of drudgery than of life.

- The priests consistently described themselves as being overworked, overburdened, and "burned out."

- The research concluded that "the main stressor is overwork and over-responsibility."

- It was apparent that the greater majority of priests were incapable of setting realistic limits.

- The priests experienced their major satisfaction in performing priestly acts that they do alone and in which they are the center of attention, such as presiding at the Eucharist, preaching, and administering the sacraments.

- They never seemed to conceive of any alternative methods for pastoral ministry, such as making sick calls, visiting nursing homes, and attending to administrative responsibilities, other than continuing to do it themselves.

- Too much work was listed as a common problem for priests, whether they are generally satisfied or not.

- One-third of each of the three categories—diocesan, religious and resigned—indicated that the theologate prepared them either not at all or not very well for working with lay staff.

What emerges from this recounting is that given these realities and with no change in pastoral approach, these priests are destined to begin an inevitable slide into exhaustion, burnout, discouragement, cynicism, and possible resignation. What is conspicuously absent throughout all the narratives is any indication of the inevitable consequences unless they choose to operate differently. Nowhere did I see any indication of the need to consider functioning in any way but the antiquated model of the "lone (and lonely) ranger." Not one of these men seemed to realize there is another option: to spend time animating the gifts of the laity and fostering collaboration. This is in spite of the clear mandate spelled out in the *Catechism of the Catholic Church:* "The ministerial priesthood is at the service of the common priesthood. It is directed at the baptismal grace of all Christians."[8]

Only when these priests choose to minister differently will they reverse this downward spiral and regain the zeal and fullness of life that must characterize any effective Christian leader. Rather, the priests depicted in this study are prime candidates for burnout. Burnout is one of the major obstacles to collaborative ministry. Burnout is not a result of the amount of work or ministry that one does; rather, it is caused by having unrealistic expectations of oneself. Burnout prevents collaborative ministry from occurring because individuals who are burned out are in reality depressed. Depressed people do not have the energy to act collaboratively or to think creatively. The model they project of the sad, tired, depressed person discourages others from being attracted to work collaboratively with them.

Jesus said that he came that we would have life and have it in abundance (John 10:10). Sadly, if there is no change in the attitudes and behaviors of these priests, if they do not begin to think and act collaboratively, we can predict that they will burn out and will not reflect the life of Jesus Christ.

Recommendations

I would like to offer a few suggestions for assisting these priests to become more effective collaborative, pastoral leaders. Although the recommendations are directed toward diocesan, congregational, and seminary leaders, it is also incumbent on the newly ordained himself to take the initiative to implement the recommendations.

- Pervasive attitudes that deter collaboration must be challenged. This is key. This should begin in the seminaries. Seminaries could devise attitudinal questionnaires to ascertain potential problems and initiate programs and personal approaches to address these issues.

- Since roughly one-third of the men felt ill-prepared to work collaboratively with laity, remedies should be developed to reverse this during the seminary years. In addition, continuing education programs for clergy, especially young clergy, should focus on developing skills and attitudes to do this. All the good will in the world is ineffective unless the priests

---

[8] *Catechism of the Catholic Church.* Vatican City: Libreria Editrice Vaticana, 1994, no. 1547.

have the personal resources to develop the skills and processes for fostering collaboration.

- Most ministers find satisfaction in "doing" for others. The more pastoral leaders are imbued with the attitude and desire to see as one of their primary goals the empowering and animating the gifts of all, the more successful collaboration will be. Moving from doer to animator is not achieved easily. It begins with a conscious change in attitude, combined with the conviction that assuming such a role will enhance the mission of Christ. Help priests to see their primary role as animator of the gifts of all rather than being the "super-doer" of ministries.

- Provide opportunities for seminarians and priests to reflect with others to help clarify those expectations that can lead to burnout. Most people do not change expectations unless they allow individuals such as friends, co-ministers, support groups, spiritual directors, counselors, or therapists to enter into their private world and assist them in evaluating whether their expectations are from God or from self and whether they are fostering or draining life.

- Seminaries and clergy continuing education programs are needed to address the issue of intimacy, loneliness, celibacy, and sexual orientation in very direct ways. Too many seminaries offer one program of this nature during the seminary years. This is inadequate. As seminarians are exposed to more experiences of ministry, new issues arise and need to be addressed in new ways. I work with one seminary that provides a program on sexuality and celibacy for all new students. Another program is required just before the seminarians begin their year of pastoral experience. Ideally, resources will also be available to help them process out their own personal journeys after such experiences.

- There is often a profound sense of loss experienced by many young priests when they leave the seminary. The narratives revealed a number of cases of individuals who were surprised by the sense of loss they experienced when they left the security, camaraderie, and affirming climate of the seminary. Failure to deal with loss is an obstacle to collaboration. Individuals who do not attend to the emotions accompanying loss usually are unwilling to invest themselves in new relationships and become pastorally ineffective. Continuing education programs for clergy should help priests address the emotions that surface at times of transition. Many dioceses attend to this at the time of transfers.

I conclude with a message of hope. Since the overwhelming majority of priests I meet are good, holy men, committed to finding the most effective ways to foster the mission of Jesus Christ, I presume that the Holy Spirit, active in the lives of the newly ordained, is propelling them in the same direction. Two things will facilitate the movement of the Spirit. First, those in leadership of seminaries, dioceses, and congregations must create a climate that is conducive to fostering personal growth. Second, the newly ordained must respond to the promptings of the Spirit and be humble enough to see their need for growth. If these two things occur, we are likely to see another generation of effective pastoral, collaborative priests.

Brother Sofield is author of numerous books on collaborative ministry. He also conducts workshops around the world on the topic.

Appendix

Table A1
Background and Description of Sample Members
(In Percents)

Number of cases:	Active Diocesan (255)	Active Religious (256)	Resigned (72)
Present age:			
29 or less	6	2	1
30–34	31	21	24
35–39	26	36	51
40–49	23	30	19
50–59	9	8	1
60 or more	5	3	3
In what year were you ordained?			
1992	0	0	35
1993	0	0	15
1994	0	0	18
1995	17	19	11
1996	23	17	8
1997	21	20	4
1998	21	21	7
1999	17	22	1
What was your age when you were ordained?			
29 or less	26	12	44
30–34	28	34	38
35–39	17	27	10
40–49	19	18	5
50–59	7	8	3
60 or more	3	1	0
Mean age of ordination	36	37	32
What was your age when you resigned?			
29 or less			7
30–34			43
35–39			33
40–49			13
50–59			1
60 or more			3
Mean age of resignation			36
Country of birth:			
U.S.A.	80	80	96
Philippines	2	2	1

Vietnam	6	6	0
Mexico	3	4	0
Eastern Europe	2	1	0
Western Europe, Ireland	3	1	0
South America	1	4	1
Central America, except Mexico	2	1	1
Other Asian	1	1	0
Other	1	0	0

How long have you been in the U.S.A.? (N = 57, 53, 3)

4 years or less	11	6	a
5–9 years	23	13	a
10–19 years	39	43	a
20 or more years	27	38	a

Where was your theologate or post-novitiate formation program?

U.S.A.	96	94	95
Philippines	0	1	0
Vietnam	1	1	0
Mexico	0	0	0
Eastern Europe	0	0	0
Western Europe, Ireland	1	2	3
South America	0	0	1
Central America, except Mexico	1	1	0
Other Asian	0	1	0
Other	0	0	1

What best describes your main racial or ethnic background?

English, Irish, Scotch, Welsh	35	29	32
Western European	29	32	42
Eastern European	7	7	15
Hispanic Background	9	12	3
Black American	0	1	0
African	1	0	0
Asian	6	8	0
Filipino	2	2	1
Mixed or other	10	8	7

Lifelong Catholic or a convert?

Lifelong Catholic	94	95	93
Convert, 3 years or less before seminary	2	1	2
Convert, 4–5 years before seminary	2	2	1
Convert, 6–10 years before seminary	2	0	1
Convert, more than 10 years before seminary	1	2	2

Table A1 (cont.)

Number of cases:	Active Diocesan (255)	Active Religious (256)	Resigned (72)
Did you have an experience of spiritual awakening in your youth or adult years?			
Yes, and it was important for my vocation	66	64	60
Yes, but it was not important for my vocation	13	9	8
No	21	27	32
If yes, at what age was it? (N = 138, 126, 42)			
14 or less	20	13	26
15–19	31	28	38
20–24	17	34	25
25–29	12	14	2
30 or more	20	11	8
Before beginning theological studies, did you attend seminary college?			
Yes, 4 years	21	17	19
Yes, 1–3 years	29	14	26
No	50	69	54
Before beginning theological studies in the seminary, did you work full-time for a year or more?			
Yes	76	80	71
No	24	20	29
If yes, for how many years?			
1–2 years	16	19	36
3–4 years	20	20	26
5–9 years	20	32	24
10–19 years	21	18	8
20 or more years	23	11	6
What was your occupation at that time?			
Engineering, computers	5	10	10
Business, management, finance, accounting	22	14	13
Christian ministry	7	7	6
Teaching	12	19	11
Professor, scientist	2	2	2

Social worker, counselor	5	9	4
Administration, assistant	5	6	10
Government, public service	3	5	8
Physician	2	1	0
Nurse or health profession	4	2	2
Lawyer	3	1	4
Sales, clerical	10	7	12
Technician, mechanical, paramedical	4	1	2
Military	7	3	10
Skilled or craftsman	8	4	8
Other	2	10	0
What was your undergraduate major?			
Humanities, philosophy	36	33	40
Religion, theology	5	7	4
Fine art, music	3	3	0
Natural science, mathematics	7	8	6
Engineering, computer science	4	5	8
Social science, psychology, history, political science	18	22	17
Business, economics, marketing, accounting	13	12	19
Education	2	3	3
Law enforcement, social work, counseling, nursing	4	3	1
Mixed or other	7	4	2
How many years total of seminary training did you have?			
4 years or less	18	22	14
5–6 years	44	28	47
7–8 years	23	23	22
9–10 years	10	12	10
11 or more years	5	14	7
Did you take time out from studies during your theological seminary years?			
Yes, 2 years or more	7	10	6
Yes, 1 year	11	6	15
No	82	84	79

a   Too few to percentage.

Table A2
How Well Did Your Theologate Prepare You?
(In Percents)

	Active Diocesan	Active Religious	Resigned
A. Formal theological training			
Very well	54	59	72
Well	41	39	25
Not very well	5	2	1
Not at all	0	0	2
B. Homiletics			
Very well	39	39	47
Well	49	47	44
Not very well	11	12	8
Not at all	1	2	0
C. Spirituality and prayer life			
Very well	30	30	42
Well	47	47	47
Not very well	21	18	11
Not at all	2	4	0
D. Understanding changes in the priesthood			
Very well	25	24	15
Well	50	44	46
Not very well	23	26	33
Not at all	2	6	6
E. Pastoral care and counseling			
Very well	36	38	36
Well	51	45	46
Not very well	12	16	18
Not at all	0	1	0
F. Church administration			
Very well	3	2	3
Well	25	17	21
Not very well	43	47	57
Not at all	29	34	19
G. Working with lay staff			
Very well	18	26	24
Well	48	42	37
Not very well	25	26	35
Not at all	9	6	4

H. Working with multiple ethnic groups

Very well	26	27	37
Well	37	37	29
Not very well	30	26	26
Not at all	7	10	7

I. Handling multiple tasks and responsibilities

Very well	23	18	19
Well	46	44	43
Not very well	25	30	32
Not at all	6	8	6

J. Balancing self-care and ministry

Very well	28	16	24
Well	51	49	50
Not very well	18	28	22
Not at all	3	7	4

K. Understanding yourself as a sexual person

Very well	31	20	25
Well	50	52	26
Not very well	15	21	35
Not at all	4	7	14

L. Developing personal support networks

Very well	25	20	22
Well	47	46	35
Not very well	24	26	40
Not at all	4	8	3

M. Handling problems of loneliness

Very well	17	9	4
Well	46	39	34
Not very well	28	38	49
Not at all	9	14	13

N. (If religious:) Preparation for the religious life

Very well	31	29
Well	46	53
Not very well	18	12
Not at all	5	6

Table A3
Experiences in the Priesthood
(In Percents)

	Active Diocesan	Active Religious	Resigned
Do you now serve in the same diocese in which you lived during your teenage years?			
Yes	52		65
No	48		35
How many priests are in your diocese?			
Under 100	31		28
100–199	37		28
200–299	12		12
300–499	11		16
500 or more	9		16
Do you now (or did you) serve in a ministry or community geographically close to where you lived during your teenage years? (N = 253, 15)			
Yes		24	47
No		76	53
How many religious are in your province? (N = 253, 15)			
Under 100		26	27
100–199		23	7
200–299		22	20
300–499		20	33
500 or more		9	13
How would you rate your first assignment after ordination in terms of helping you make the transition from seminary to priestly ministry?			
Very helpful	46	42	24
Helpful	32	32	23
Not too helpful	12	22	31
Detrimental	10	4	22
Why was it helpful or not helpful? (up to 2 ideas coded)			
Positive:			
Supportive, understanding pastor	44	13	22
Supportive parishioners	14	12	4
Supportive priests (other than pastor)	2	4	10
Good transition process	3	8	7
Good parish, active parish	7	7	7
Good pace of work, not overburdened	2	4	3

Could carry out my sacramental priestly role	3	10	1
Good opportunities, good fulfillment	12	18	5
Large parish	7	3	5
Small parish	1	1	0
Familiar setting	1	5	1

Negative:

Unsupportive pastor, problem pastor	19	5	33
Unsupportive parishioners	0	0	3
Unsupportive priests (other than pastor)	0	2	3
Poor transition process	3	6	8
Few opportunities to carry out my sacramental priestly role	0	3	4
Few opportunities for fulfillment	0	3	3
No mentor; absence of pastor	1	3	1
Little privacy, too public, too much action	1	2	10
Different role than I was trained for	1	4	5
Other	2	1	1

Have you been involved in a formal mentoring program after ordination?

Yes	39	20	40
No	61	80	60

(If yes:) Was it helpful?

Very helpful	34	49	14
Helpful	41	42	38
Not too helpful	25	5	48
Detrimental	0	4	0

What is your current ministerial position?

Pastor	21	7
Parochial vicar	66	35
Full-time administration	3	7
Educational apostolate	3	28
Hospital or prison chaplaincy	1	1
Ministry with a special group	1	7
Other	4	15

Do you (or did you) have enough freedom and authority to make decisions in carrying out your ministry?

Yes	86	87	68
No	14	13	32

Table A3 (cont.)

	Active Diocesan	Active Religious	Resigned
(If no:) Explain: (N = 37, 34, 22)			
Pastor made all decisions	57	35	36
Pastor was easily threatened	11	9	18
Too functionary	3	3	9
Not part of planning process	11	17	4
Could only make suggestions	5	15	18
All decisions were made by religious community	5	12	5
Other	8	9	9
Were you satisfied or dissatisfied with your living situation in your first assignment?			
Very satisfied	49	41	18
Somewhat satisfied	24	30	35
Somewhat dissatisfied	11	13	21
Very dissatisfied	15	15	25
Don't know, or other	1	1	1
Why were you satisfied or dissatisfied?			
Positive:			
Personal privacy	8	2	6
Living quarters separate from office	3	3	0
Comfortable space, ample	14	3	8
Had practical needs met	3	3	4
Liked urban environment	1	2	0
Agreeable priests, pastor	18	8	7
Had own home, apartment	3	0	1
Good community life	3	31	11
Negative:			
Living quarters inadequate	3	1	1
Lack of personal privacy	12	3	14
Living quarters too close to office	6	1	13
Problems with priests, pastor	11	16	15
Felt like guest in pastor's house	3	2	7
Lack of community life	2	10	7
Didn't like community life	1	4	1
Church, community too small	0	3	0
Other	9	7	3

Are you satisfied or dissatisfied with your living situation now?

Very satisfied	60	45
Somewhat satisfied	23	35
Somewhat dissatisfied	8	12
Very dissatisfied	7	6
Don't know, or other	2	2

Why are you satisfied or dissatisfied?

Positive:

Personal privacy	8	5
Living quarters separate from office	6	2
Comfortable space	11	3
Ample quarters	7	1
Had practical needs met	4	6
Liked urban environment	1	0
Agreeable priests, pastor	16	6
Have own home, apartment	9	3
Good community life	5	30

Negative:

Living quarters inadequate	1	1
Lack of personal privacy	6	4
Living quarters too close to office	5	2
Problems with priests, pastor	8	12
Feel like guest in pastor's house	2	0
Lack of community life	3	7
Don't like community life	1	2
Church, community too small	0	3
Other	8	14

Table A4
Sources of Satisfaction?
(In Percents)

	Active Diocesan	Active Religious	Resigned
How important is each as a source of satisfaction to you?			
A. Administering the sacraments and presiding over the liturgy			
Great importance	97	92	85
Some importance	3	6	12
Little importance	0	1	3
No importance	0	0	0
B. Administering the life of the Church			
Great importance	46	30	35
Some importance	42	48	47
Little importance	10	18	17
No importance	1	4	1
C. Security that your vocation is a response to the divine call			
Great importance	72	54	47
Some importance	22	35	32
Little importance	5	11	17
No importance	1	0	4
D. Preaching the Word			
Great importance	89	87	90
Some importance	10	12	7
Little importance	0	1	3
No importance	0	0	0
E. Being respected as a leader of Christians			
Great importance	37	28	35
Some importance	46	44	43
Little importance	15	23	15
No importance	2	5	7
F. The opportunity to work with many people and be a part of their lives			
Great importance	75	74	82
Some importance	23	24	18
Little importance	2	2	0
No importance	0	0	0
G. Living the common life with like-minded priests or members of your religious community			
Great importance	27	62	26
Some importance	39	28	38
Little importance	22	8	17
No importance	12	2	19

H. Being a visible sign of the Catholic Church

Great importance	54	47	28
Some importance	35	36	43
Little importance	11	13	24
No importance	0	4	5

I. Helping people and families in their daily lives

Great importance	79	76	82
Some importance	21	22	15
Little importance	0	2	3
No importance	0	0	0

At present, what is your level of satisfaction with the following?

A. Current work in ministry

Very satisfied	72	61	43
Somewhat satisfied	25	27	36
Somewhat dissatisfied	2	11	10
Very dissatisfied	1	1	11

B. Your living situation

Very satisfied	58	46	24
Somewhat satisfied	26	32	33
Somewhat dissatisfied	9	16	18
Very dissatisfied	7	6	25

C. Spiritual life

Very satisfied	31	26	21
Somewhat satisfied	52	56	40
Somewhat dissatisfied	15	16	31
Very dissatisfied	2	2	8

D. Personal time schedule

Very satisfied	26	18	14
Somewhat satisfied	51	49	36
Somewhat dissatisfied	18	27	32
Very dissatisfied	4	6	18

E. Living a celibate life

Very satisfied	53	33	7
Somewhat satisfied	34	41	23
Somewhat dissatisfied	9	19	28
Very dissatisfied	4	7	42

F. Opportunities for continuing education

Very satisfied	28	32	26
Somewhat satisfied	42	45	43
Somewhat dissatisfied	24	18	14
Very dissatisfied	6	5	17

Table A4 (cont.)

	Active Diocesan	Active Religious	Resigned
G. The support you receive from fellow priests			
Very satisfied	39	30	19
Somewhat satisfied	41	48	44
Somewhat dissatisfied	15	19	19
Very dissatisfied	5	3	17
H. Your relationship with the bishop or superior			
Very satisfied	48	44	22
Somewhat satisfied	39	41	39
Somewhat dissatisfied	10	11	17
Very dissatisfied	3	4	22
I. Your relationship with the laity with whom you work			
Very satisfied	73	67	67
Somewhat satisfied	25	30	24
Somewhat dissatisfied	2	2	8
Very dissatisfied	0	1	1
J. Fairness and openness in chancery decisions			
Very satisfied	24	25	14
Somewhat satisfied	46	51	30
Somewhat dissatisfied	19	16	23
Very dissatisfied	11	8	33

Table A5
Problems Which Priests Face Today
(In Percents)

	Active Diocesan	Active Religious	Resigned
A. Lack of agreement on what a priest is			
A great problem	8	7	17
Somewhat of a problem	26	34	44
Very little problem	33	36	17
No problem	33	23	22
B. Difficulty of establishing private living space			
A great problem	10	9	36
Somewhat of a problem	22	29	28
Very little problem	31	35	12
No problem	37	27	24
C. Unrealistic demands and expectations of lay people			
A great problem	10	9	24
Somewhat of a problem	42	46	33
Very little problem	39	35	28
No problem	9	10	15
D. Being a public person all the time			
A great problem	9	11	31
Somewhat of a problem	37	48	43
Very little problem	37	31	19
No problem	17	10	7
E. Loneliness of priestly life			
A great problem	8	18	46
Somewhat of a problem	29	39	37
Very little problem	38	30	14
No problem	24	13	3
F. Living a celibate life			
A great problem	7	13	47
Somewhat of a problem	25	40	35
Very little problem	43	36	10
No problem	25	11	8
G. Too much work			
A great problem	13	24	28
Somewhat of a problem	45	42	22
Very little problem	32	27	18
No problem	10	7	32

H. Disagreements with other priests over ecclesiology and ministry

A great problem	12	9	21
Somewhat of a problem	30	29	35
Very little problem	38	45	23
No problem	20	17	21

I. The way authority is too lax in the Church

A great problem	6	2	4
Somewhat of a problem	18	12	6
Very little problem	42	33	14
No problem	34	53	76

J. The way authority is too heavy-handed in the Church

A great problem	3	16	34
Somewhat of a problem	14	35	37
Very little problem	45	32	8
No problem	38	17	21

K. Your relationship with your pastor

A great problem	8	6	18
Somewhat of a problem	14	11	23
Very little problem	25	31	13
No problem	53	52	46

L. Your relationship with your bishop or major superior

A great problem	2	3	14
Somewhat of a problem	13	9	31
Very little problem	30	33	19
No problem	55	55	36

M. Inadequate salary and benefits

A great problem	7	4	11
Somewhat of a problem	18	12	21
Very little problem	27	19	14
No problem	48	65	54

N. Difficulty of really reaching people today

A great problem	5	5	7
Somewhat of a problem	33	32	22
Very little problem	40	36	24
No problem	22	27	47

O. Being expected to represent Church teachings you have difficulty with

A great problem	4	12	22
Somewhat of a problem	12	28	42
Very little problem	39	43	10
No problem	45	17	26

Table A6
Attitudes about the Priesthood and the Church Today
(In Percents)

	Active Diocesan	Active Religious	Resigned
Catholic laity need to be better educated to respect the authority of the priest's word			
Strongly agree	10	5	1
Moderately agree	26	11	8
Uncertain	19	13	6
Moderately disagree	30	32	28
Strongly disagree	15	39	57
A priest must see himself as a "man set apart" by God			
Strongly agree	34	12	6
Moderately agree	35	28	22
Uncertain	7	9	11
Moderately disagree	16	30	15
Strongly disagree	8	21	46
Ordination confers on the priest a new status which makes him essentially different from the laity			
Strongly agree	44	18	10
Moderately agree	31	34	17
Uncertain	6	7	6
Moderately disagree	10	21	26
Strongly disagree	9	20	42
Celibacy should be an option for diocesan priests			
Strongly agree	16	42	79
Moderately agree	13	22	15
Uncertain	16	15	3
Moderately disagree	15	8	1
Strongly disagree	40	13	1
The Catholic Church should allow women greater participation in all ministries			
Strongly agree	22	50	79
Moderately agree	23	25	11
Uncertain	17	9	3
Moderately disagree	22	10	6
Strongly disagree	16	7	1

It is essential to make the distinction between priests and laity more important in the Church

Strongly agree	13	6	4
Moderately agree	30	18	4
Uncertain	19	10	4
Moderately disagree	21	35	26
Strongly disagree	17	31	61

Priests today should be given much more freedom to choose their living arrangements

Strongly agree	23	15	51
Moderately agree	28	26	21
Uncertain	17	31	17
Moderately disagree	22	20	11
Strongly disagree	10	8	0

Priests today should be given much more say in choosing their assignments

Strongly agree	15	18	44
Moderately agree	35	41	31
Uncertain	17	21	10
Moderately disagree	26	19	11
Strongly disagree	7	1	4

Priests today should be more involved with broad social issues

Strongly agree	31	52	65
Moderately agree	43	32	24
Uncertain	11	9	3
Moderately disagree	13	6	6
Strongly disagree	2	1	3

Table A7
The Decision to Resign
(In Percents)

	Active Diocesan	Active Religious	Resigned
When did you first think seriously about leaving the priesthood?			
Before ordination			32
After ordination			68
Which of the following statements reflects your feelings about your future in the priesthood?			
I definitely will not leave.	71	58	
I probably will not leave.	24	28	
I am uncertain about my future.	4	11	
I probably will leave.	1	2	
I have definitely decided to leave.	0	1	
What were your main motivations to resign? (up to 2 ideas coded)			
Fell in love; wanted marriage or intimate relationship with a woman			42
Celibacy was a problem			26
Dissatisfaction with Church administration or trends			16
Loneliness was a problem			15
As a gay person, was not understood or supported			7
Left because of illness			7
Little room to express personal gifts or talents			7
Overwhelmed with demands of superiors			5
Overwhelmed with responsibilities toward parishioners			4
Discouragement with fellow priests			4
Discomfort with theological issues			4
Feared alcoholism or other unhealthy escape			3
Other			5

Are (were) you satisfied or dissatisfied with the help and support you receive from priests with more years of service?

Very satisfied	42	35	25
Somewhat satisfied	39	41	32
Somewhat dissatisfied	11	16	21
Very dissatisfied	5	6	17
Don't know, or other	2	2	5

Are (were) you satisfied or dissatisfied with peer support you have (had) from other priests in your diocese or community who were ordained at about the same time?

Very satisfied	41	32	22
Somewhat satisfied	36	40	32
Somewhat dissatisfied	14	14	22
Very dissatisfied	5	7	19
Don't know, or other	4	7	4

Additional Resources

Here we describe the main psychological, sociological, and historical works that we know of on newly ordained priests to assist researchers and Church leaders. The theological literature is beyond our scope in these pages except as it is referred to in other works; we limit ourselves to empirical studies. The research can best be categorized under six headings.

1. *Seminaries.* Numerous works have been written about Catholic seminaries and seminarians, and two journals are devoted to them: *Seminary Journal* and *Seminaries in Dialogue.* The most important book is *Seminaries, Theologates, and the Future of Church Ministry* (1999) by Katarina Schuth. Schuth received a grant to visit all forty-two seminaries to interview rectors, faculty, and students, and to carry out surveys. The book contains a review of earlier studies.

2. *Newly Ordained Priests.* We need to mention the most thorough sociological study of American priests ever done, that carried out by Andrew Greeley and associates in 1970 and reported on in *The Catholic Priest in the United States: Sociological Investigations* (1972a). The book looks at numerous facets of priestly life, including work life, spirituality, satisfactions and frustrations, morale, and future plans. It includes a sample of resigned as well as active priests. Greeley also published a short book of commentary on the state of the priesthood, *Priests in the United States: Reflections on a Survey* (1972b). Although the two Greeley books are not solely devoted to newly ordained priests, they contain rich information on them.

At the same time that Greeley and his associates were engaged in a sociological survey of priests, Eugene Kennedy and Victor Heckler were making a major study of the psychology of priests. It eventuated in *The Catholic Priest in the United States: Psychological Investigations* (1972), a book that has been very influential.

An incisive but somewhat unknown volume, *The First Year of Priesthood* (1978), was written by David O'Rourke. It analyzes the most common first-year experiences of priests. O'Rourke describes three kinds of first years: the "sink-or-swim model," the "domesticating model," and the "apprenticeship model."

In 1990 Eugene Hemrick and Dean Hoge carried out a nationwide survey of priests ordained between five and nine years. Entitled *A Survey of Priests Ordained Five to Nine Years* (1991), the report is mainly on the priests' evaluations of seminary training and the transition to priesthood.

NOCERCC (the National Organization for Continuing Education of Roman Catholic Clergy, Inc.) commissioned Dean Hoge in 1998 to compile and review all existing research on newly ordained priests. The compilation and responses by four NOCERCC members was published as a short book in 1999, *Expressed Needs and Attitudes of Newly Ordained Priests.*

3. *Resigned Priests.* As noted above, the first high-quality study of resigned priests was done by Andrew Greeley and associates in 1970. It looked only at those who resigned in the period January 1966 through December 1969, a time characterized by a high resignation rate (see Greeley, 1972a, chap. 15). Since the Greeley study, no large-scale studies of resignees have been made, to our knowledge; we know only of clinical studies.

4. *Sexual Issues.* We know of a dozen recent books on sexual issues facing priests, the majority of which are on priestly misconduct and lie outside our present concern. The most influential book on sexuality of priests is A. W. Richard Sipe's *A Secret World* (1990). It summarizes Sipe's findings from years of psychoanalytic practice helping priests. The book has been criticized as not being based on any random sample, but Sipe rightly argues that random samples on such sensitive topics are impossible. His main conclusions are credible, even given the imprecision.

A book on homosexuality, James Wolf's *Gay Priests* (1989), includes observations by informed observers and several personal life histories.

5. *Priestly Morale and Well-Being.* An important article, "Reflections on the Morale of Priests," was written by a committee of priests and published in *Origins* (a Catholic newsletter of documents) in 1989. It has been influential because of its twenty-odd concrete recommendations.

A recent article, based on conclusions of a task force of pastors, was authored by Thomas Sweetser and published in *America* magazine, July 2–9, 2001, entitled "A Letter to the American Catholic Bishops from Your Pastors." It analyzes pressures on priests today and makes practical recommendations to the bishops.

Raymond Hedin's *Married to the Church* (1995) is an insightful book. Hedin is a former seminarian who was never ordained and who about twenty years later talked at length with his former classmates, both active priests and men who had resigned. The accounts convey the priests' experiences, especially their joys and sorrows.

The most read book on the priesthood in recent years has been Donald Cozzens's *The Changing Face of the Priesthood* (2000). Cozzens, a long-time Catholic seminary rector, reflects on his experiences and asks for more open discussion of celibacy, homosexuality, and clericalism. The book contains reviews of research.

A useful volume was published in 1995 by a group of researchers who interviewed thirty-five priests nominated as effective and exemplary. Entitled *Grace Under Pressure: What Gives Life to American Priests* (edited by James Walsh et al.), it conveys the spiritual strength and fervor of these men.

6. *Trends in the Priesthood.* Three books need to be mentioned. The first, *Full Pews, Empty Altars,* by Richard Schoenherr and Lawrence Young (1993), is the most reliable analysis of trends in numbers of priests in the United States. Schoenherr and Young use actuarial methods to analyze the priest shortage and project the future.

A recent compilation of trend data by Bryan Froehle and Mary Gautier, *Catholicism USA* (2000), is a good sourcebook of data on Catholic institutions, including trends in seminaries and priests.

Finally, an influential book by Philip Murnion and David DeLambo, *Parishes and Parish Ministers: A Study of Parish Lay Ministry* (1999), depicts changes in parish life during the 1990s, including the rising numbers and increasing influence of professional lay ministers. It clarifies future priestly roles in parish leadership.

References

Cozzens, Donald B. 2000. *The Changing Face of the Priesthood*. Collegeville, Minn.: Liturgical Press.

Cuijpers, Pim, Yvonne Langendoen, and Rob V. Bijl. 1999. "Psychiatric Disorders in Adult Children of Problem Drinkers." *Addiction* 94:10–19.

Daly, William P. 2001. "Early Career Resignations from the Priesthood." Report. Cincinnati, Ohio: National Association of Church Personnel Administrators.

D'Antonio, William V., James D. Davidson, Dean R. Hoge, and Katherine Meyer. 2001. *American Catholics: Gender, Generation, and Commitment*. Walnut Creek, Calif.: AltaMira Press.

Farley, Reynolds. 1996. *The New American Reality*. New York: Russell Sage Foundation.

Froehle, Bryan T., and Mary L. Gautier. 2000. *Catholicism USA: A Portrait of the Catholic Church in the United States*. Maryknoll, N.Y.: Orbis Books.

Greeley, Andrew M. 1972a. *The Catholic Priest in the United States: Sociological Investigations*. Washington: United States Catholic Conference.

————. 1972b. *Priests in the United States: Reflections on a Survey*. New York: Doubleday.

Hedin, Raymond. 1995. *Married to the Church*. Bloomington, Ind.: Indiana University Press.

Hemrick, Eugene F., and Dean R. Hoge. 1985. *Seminarians in Theology: A National Profile*. Washington: National Conference of Catholic Bishops.

————. 1991. *A Survey of Priests Ordained Five to Nine Years*. Washington: National Catholic Educational Association.

Hennessy, Paul K., ed. 1997. *A Concert of Charisms: Ordained Ministry in Religious Life*. New York: Paulist Press.

Hoge, Dean R. 1999. *Expressed Needs and Attitudes of Newly Ordained Priests*. Booklet, with Responses by NOCERCC Members. Chicago: National Organization for Continuing Education of Roman Catholic Clergy.

Hoge, Dean R., Raymond H. Potvin, and Kathleen M. Ferry. 1984. *Research on Men's Vocations to the Priesthood and the Religious Life*. Washington: United States Catholic Conference.

Johnson, Jeannette L., and Linda A. Bennett. 1989. *Adult Children of Alcoholics: Theory and Research.* New Brunswick, N.J.: Rutgers Center of Alcohol Studies.

Kenna, Joseph. 2000. "The Psychology of Intimacy in the Diocesan Priesthood." Unpublished Dissertation, Union Institute Graduate College.

Kennedy, Eugene C. 2001. *The Unhealed Wound: The Church and Human Sexuality.* New York: St. Martin's Press.

Kennedy, Eugene C., and Victor J. Heckler. 1972. *The Catholic Priest in the United States: Psychological Investigations.* Washington: United States Catholic Conference.

Martin, James I. 1995. "Intimacy, Loneliness, and Openness to Feelings in Adult Children of Alcoholics." *Health and Social Work* 20:52–60.

Murnion, Philip J., and David DeLambo. 1999. *Parishes and Parish Ministers: A Study of Parish Lay Ministry.* New York: National Pastoral Life Center.

National Conference of Catholic Bishops Committee on Priestly Life and Ministry. 1989. "Reflections on the Morale of Priests." *Origins* (January 12) 497–505.

Nestor, Thomas F. 1993. "Intimacy and Adjustment Among Catholic Priests." Unpublished Ph.D. Dissertation, Loyola University of Chicago.

O'Rourke, David K. 1978. *The First Year of Priesthood.* Huntington, Ind.: Our Sunday Visitor Press.

Page, Penny Booth. 1991. *Children of Alcoholics: A Sourcebook.* New York: Garland.

Putnam, Robert D. 2000. *Bowling Alone: The Collapse and Revival of American Community.* New York: Simon and Schuster.

Schoenherr, Richard A., and Andrew M. Greeley. 1974. "Role Commitment Processes and the American Catholic Priesthood." *American Sociological Review* 39:407–426.

Schoenherr, Richard A., and Lawrence A. Young. 1993. *Full Pews and Empty Altars.* Madison, Wis.: University of Wisconsin Press.

Schuth, Katarina. 1999. *Seminaries, Theologates, and the Future of Church Ministry.* Collegeville, Minn.: Liturgical Press.

Seidler, John. 1979. "Priest Resignations in a Lazy Monopoly." *American Sociological Review* 44:763–783.

Shields, Joseph J., and Mary Jeanne Verdieck. 1985. *Religious Life in the United States: The Experience of Men's Communities.* Report. Washington: Center for Applied Research in the Apostolate.

Sipe, A. W. Richard. 1990. *A Secret World: Sexuality and the Search for Celibacy.* New York: Brunner/Mazel.

Sweetser, Thomas P. 2001. "A Letter to the American Catholic Bishops from Your Pastors." *America* (July 2–9) 18–20.

Walsh, James, et al. 1995. *Grace Under Pressure: What Gives Life to American Priests.* Washington: National Catholic Educational Association.

Wheeler, Barbara G. 2001. "Fit for Ministry? A New Profile of Seminarians." *Christian Century* (April 11) 16–23.

Wolf, James G., ed. 1989. *Gay Priests.* San Francisco: Harper and Row.

Index